How to Write A Screenplay

Revised and Expanded

Mark Evan Schwartz

earn to write a screenplay by reading one

continuum

HOW TO WRITE:
A SCREENPLAY
Revised and Expanded

by
Mark Evan Schwartz

continuum

NEW YORK • LONDON

2007

The Continuum International Publishing Group Inc
80 Maiden Lane, New York, NY 10038

The Continuum International Publishing Group Ltd
The Tower Building, 11 York Road, London SE1 7NX

www.continuumbooks.com

Printed in the United States of America

Library of Congress Cataloging-in-Publication Data

Schwartz, Mark Evan.
    How to write : a screenplay / Mark Evan Schwartz.—revised and expanded ed.
    p.   cm.
    ISBN-13: 978-0-8264-2817-2 (pbk. : alk. paper)
    ISBN-10: 0-8264-2817-7 (pbk. : alk. paper)
    1. Motion picture authorship.   I. Title.
PN1996.S355   2007
808.2'3—dc22

2007002047

Contents

This book is dedicated to the people in my life that matter most: my family.

I'd like to thank my beautiful wife Caryl, for standing by through thick and thin, for the sacrifices she's made while I pursue my dreams, and best of all, for the ongoing love and passion we share . . . my wonderful children Allyson, Stacie, and Jared, the windows through which I see so much of the world, the mirrors in which I see so much of myself . . . my mother, who was and still is my favorite teacher . . . and my father, who passed away just days before I received word this book would be published. His belief, forever unwavered, continues to inspire.

This book was partially written with a grant from Loyola Marymount University. I'd like to extend my deep appreciation and gratitude to the faculty, administration, staff, and students of its School of Film and Television, for giving me a shelter from the storm, a place to teach so I can learn.

And to David Barker, my editor at Continuum, I'd like to offer a special tip-of-the-hat for his enthusiastic support of the unconventional.

Introduction
Merging Content with Context

Books on screenwriting flood the market, crowding shelves in libraries and bookstores, cluttering the desks of people with sure-fire movie ideas burning in their heads. As a professor at Loyola Marymount University School of Film and Television in Los Angeles, I've read, skimmed, or browsed through many of them. And as a working screenwriter, and former development exec, I can honestly say that some are quite good. But there is a common problem I've had with virtually every one I've taken the time to look at, and that is the very nature of how they are written: as books. While the best lay out matters pertaining to the art and craft of screenwriting clearly and intelligently, they remain as much of an abstraction as learning horseback riding without a horse. Just as a textbook does not look or feel like an animal, a typical "how-to" book does not look or feel like a screenplay.

So how does one create a how-to book that looks and feels like a screenplay? By writing an atypical one.

Differing from all the other manuals, *How to Write: A Screenplay* culminates in just that, an actual screenplay. Maintaining a narrative thread, it follows steps used to develop and write a first draft in the standardized format of a bound, feature-length script. Instead of laying out topics chapter by chapter like a textbook, it progresses scene by scene, with a protagonist pursuing specific objectives, coming into conflict with an antagonist generating obstacles. It has a dramatic three-act structure, with dialogue, character development, and descriptive action functioning to propel the plot. All working together to unfold and reveal a cinematic story that illustrates the basic elements of screenwriting.

In short, it looks like a movie script, feels like a movie script, and reads like a movie script. And therein lies its greatest significance. By merging content with context, it makes learning the art and craft of screenwriting more accessible.

The inspiration for this approach comes from my classroom experience. Rather than giving students a handout listing where and how to place scene headings, slug lines, character, dialogue, parentheticals, and various forms of descriptive action on the page, I pass out a short script I wrote titled "Good Format Hunting." In it, two oppositional characters charge through a series of scenes, discussing, arguing, and cajoling about matters related to screenplay format as it simultaneously appears on the page they inhabit. My students clearly respond to the script, laughing while reading it, bringing it to class from week to week, keeping it at their sides as a reference tool while writing. Their work radically improves, becoming more professional looking as a result of it. Several students, telling me how valuable they've found it, suggested I try to get it published. I thought, why not? But instead of just a short script about format, I should create an entire screenplay about how to write one. Hence, this project was born.

In that good screenwriting details action, not explanation, I'll take a moment to explain how it all works before we get started.

The first section of *How to Write: A Screenplay* functions to demonstrate and exemplify some suggested steps of creative development. Tools, if you will, to help you construct a working cinematic story, precursors to the writing of the script. You might find it desirable to use all five of these steps, or perhaps just some of them. Then again, you might choose to forsake the whole kit and caboodle and dive directly into drafting your screenplay, modeled in the second and most substantial part of this book. The only part, in fact, that ultimately matters. Because the screenplay is what you take to market, with any luck option or sell, and, miracle of miracles in the best of all possible worlds, get made.

Prior to committing to the arduous task of drafting their screenplay, some writers go out and pitch, hoping to find collaborative support and financial backing. To show how to do it, before advancing to the five steps, I've written a short script titled THE PITCH. In it, an imagined screenwriter (not to be confused with the real-life me) prepares, receives advice, and pitches a concept for a screenplay that happens to be the one created for this book. Like everything else in *How to Write: A Screenplay*, it's an attempt to avoid weighty explanation, and deliver instead a cohesive lesson by means of cinematic storytelling.

You have to decide what works best for you. Whether pitching before drafting or writing on spec, I know that going through the five steps, or variations of them depending on the project, is what works best for me. But as the saying goes: you can lead a horse to water . . . well, you get the idea.

Step one is the LOG LINE. Clearly stated in one complex sentence, it gives the gist of the cinematic concept and story. Why one sentence? Because it forces a discipline, demanding that you come to terms with specifically what it is you're intending to write. Does it mean that you're married to the approach? No. But it means you at least have to start thinking seriously about your engagement.

Next comes the SYNOPSIS, an extremely concise, three-paragraph, three-act summary of the story as it now plays in your head. By necessity, it is overly generalized, and often vague. More often than not, like the log line it will change, either completely or moderately, during the creative process of constructing the story. Then what is its value, this early in the process? Use it as a tool to begin organized thought, to further your focus on the conceptual flow of your narrative.

CHARACTER PROFILES follow. A laundry list, if you will, of aspects of the personal histories, traits, and nuances of the people in your story. After all, dramatic stories are about characters with problems and how they attempt to solve them. Allow yourself to fully envision these individuals, right from the start. Come to terms with their specific needs and fears and quirks. Flesh them out as humanly as possible, in ways that your intended audience can relate. By doing so, you'll give yourself the resources to generate empathy. And empathy is an absolute necessity. Because your audience needs to feel, and understand, the problems your characters are facing if they're going to connect with your story.

Will you use all the items on your list in the construction of your story? Probably not. It could overly complicate, contrive, and clutter your narrative flow. Do you have to stick with the choices you've made? Of course not. As ideas related to your story deepen, so should your thoughts regarding character. Then why bother? As with the synopsis, to fuel your imagination. The better you know your characters, the more vividly and truthfully you'll be able to create the universe they inhabit.

That universe begins to take shape in the fourth step, a form of outlining known as a BEAT SHEET. Concise phrases, simple sentences, and marginal thoughts notating your story's essential beats of action as you continue to envision them. Scribble them on scene cards (index cards) and tack them to a board, or list them in a word processing file in your computer. Whichever way you choose to record them, what's most important is that their arrangement be kept flexible, movable. Because you should think of them as the dramatic threads you're still choosing, still organizing, to weave together the structural tapestry that is taking shape as your story.

Substantially expanding on the beat sheet, that tapestry is a detailed prose outline referred to as a TREATMENT, perhaps the most difficult and important step in the creative development process. A further, much deeper discipline, the treatment pushes you to more fully visualize the screen story materializing in your mind's eye and, by merging structure with character, the all-important emotions stirring in your gut. Whereas a beat sheet by nature reads cold, turn up the heat with your treatment. Make it hot.

Consider pacing. A feature-length narrative story might have as few as twenty, or as many as fifty scenes, depending on scope and momentum, with each of those scenes building off of what precedes it, generating rising tension for those that will follow. For every scene in the story you're creating, your treatment should have a block paragraph that does the same. The treatment for the screenplay in this manual, for example, has only about twenty-five scenes, because of its emphasis on the relationship between its two leading characters. If, on the other hand, the screenplay were an action adventure, it'd probably have twice that many scenes, emphasizing accelerating events.

Explore tone and genre. If you're writing a comedy, your treatment should be funny. If your story is a thriller, it should put you on the edge of your seat. If it's a romance, it should tug at the heartstrings. Because of its potential significance as a tool for story construction, make your treatment a good read. Have the courage to let yourself feel what you're writing. You'll begin the process of transferring those emotions to the page.

With both the beat sheet and the treatment, like everything else up to this point in your creative process, I can't emphasize enough that choices should in no way be set in stone. Give yourself the freedom to cut and paste, arranging and rearranging as you see fit. Use the outline to provide direction, a course of action, a point of reference that will keep you from wandering too far astray as you broaden your horizons. You might find an event in act one works better in act two, or a situation in act three is excess baggage that distracts and should be eliminated. Empower yourself to evaluate yourself before you begin drafting your screenplay. It's far easier to juggle scene cards tacked to a board, or block paragraphs in your computer, than it is to rethink and reconfigure a hundred and ten pages of script.

By zeroing in on structure, plotting, beats of action, and nuances of character, solving as many narrative dilemmas as possible in advance, you'll have more freedom to explore. And while the outline is obviously not the first draft of your script, think of it as the first draft of your story. A road map. Couple it with an inventive openness to detour, and you'll more confidently embark on a fantastic journey.

And the journey that puts it all together is your SCREENPLAY. Incorporate the preceding tools; put them to work. They'll make your life easier while you strive to meet the very specific demands that are essential to crafting a narrative motion picture script. At the same time, as stated with all of the above, keep your mind open to new, fresh, unexpected ideas. Don't be committed to anything you've previously written. They're all early choices. Having made them, stronger, bolder, more exciting and original ones potentially follow.

But only if you allow the creative beast inside you to rage and howl.

How, you might ask, is *How to Write: A Screenplay* best used? Big question, simple answer: use it as a companion piece. Make it your spouse, your pet, your partner in creativity. If you're in the classroom, lecture hall, or with your writer's group, use it to stimulate discussion. If you're reading one of the many other how-to books, use it for comparison. If you're at your desk daydreaming, conceptualizing, or . . . wonder of wonders . . . writing, use it as a guide for illumination.

And above all else, use it to spark the precious fire of imagination.

I would like to acknowledge some of the excellent screenwriting books that I've found useful in the classroom as well as in the creation of this manual:

The Screenwriter's Bible by David Trotter, Silman-James Press
The Writer's Journey by Christopher Vogel, Michael Wiese Productions
Myth & the Movies by Stuart Voytilla, Michael Wiese Productions
Secrets of Screenplay Structure by Linda J. Cowgill, iFilm Publishing
This Business of Screenwriting by Ron Suppa, Esq., Lone Eagle Publishing
Screenwriting by Richard Walter, Plume Books
Screenplay by Syd Field, Delta Books
Story by Robert McKee, Regan Books

And that great-great-great-great-great-great-granddaddy of all screenwriting how-to books:

Poetics by Aristotle

Before reading the rest of this manual, I recommend viewing, or re-viewing, the movies Gladiator, Tootsie, *and* Die Hard. *Referred to throughout the text, I've chosen them for their familiarity, accessibility, and clarity of vision.*

One other thing: got to give your baby a name. And I've given one to the screenplay you are about to read. *Screenwriting for the Hell of It.* Does that give you an indication of its tone? Does it give you a clue to what it's about, while tickling your curiosity to find out more? Good. Then the title serves its function as well.

Without further explanation, because that wouldn't be good screenwriting, let's dive right in. Water's great. Hope you enjoy the swim!

THE PITCH

an original screenplay

by

Mark Evan Schwartz

Contact:

Mark Evan Schwartz
Loyola Marymount University
School of Film & Television
One LMU Drive
Los Angeles, CA 90045-2659

INT. SHOWER STALL — MORNING

Pounding water. Steam swirls, misting the translucent
stall, silhouetting someone mumbling.

                    SCREENWRITER
               (to himself)
          Okay, okay. Character, conflict, genre.
          Character, conflict, genre. Got them down,
          three key elements of the pitch. Character,
          conflict, and genre . . .

The shower's turned off.

INT. BATHROOM — MORNING

A hand wipes across a clouded mirror, revealing the
smudged reflection of a soaking wet

SCREENWRITER

In his mid-twenties. Hair plastered to his forehead,
towel wrapped around his waist, he looks himself
straight in the eye. A flicker of anxiety.

                    SCREENWRITER
          So, uh, there's this writer, see. He is a,
          you know, a screenwriter. And he, he—

                    REFLECTION
          Wait!

Screenwriter startles.

His REFLECTION suddenly takes on a life of its own,
grimaces.

                    REFLECTION
          Man, put a break on it.

Screenwriter, shaken, falls silent.

                    REFLECTION
          First of all, I don't see. Second of all, I
          don't know. And third . . . Stop stammering!
          How am I supposed to buy into your story if
          you can't even show confidence in yourself!?

                    SCREENWRITER
          Well, that's why I'm practicing my pitch.

                    REFLECTION
          With me?

                    SCREENWRITER
     With myself.

His reflection sarcastically chortles.

                    REFLECTION
     Like myself is really gonna get caught up in
     all the unpredictable twists and turns of my
     story.

                    SCREENWRITER
     Guess I'm not going to say anything I haven't
     heard before, am I?

                    REFLECTION
     Don't miss a trick, do you?

Screenwriter rubs his chin. A moment of introspection.

                    REFLECTION
     There's nothing wrong with going over it in
     front of a mirror. Good way to work on your
     appearance.

Screenwriter smoothes back his wet hair. Effects a
cocky grin and swagger.

                    REFLECTION
     But find someone fresh to the concept. Try it
     out on them, gauge their reactions.

INT. KITCHEN — MORNING

A blood-curdling scream.

                    BABY
     WHHHAAAA!!!!

Casually dressed in jeans and a nice shirt, the
Screenwriter gestures enthusiastically.

                    SCREENWRITER
     They turn! And find themselves surrounded by
     an army of salivating flesh-eating zombies!

Still in her robe, pretty in spite of disheveled hair and
bags under her eyes, his WIFE struggles to spoon-feed
their three month old colicky BABY, wailing in her
highchair.

                    SCREENWRITER
     Well? What do you think so far?

                        BABY
        WHHHAAAAA!!!!

Wife manages a tired smile.

                        WIFE
        Cute.

                        BABY
        WHHHAAAAA!!!!

                        SCREENWRITER
            (taken aback)
        Dudes're about to be K-rationed for brunch.
        And you think it's cute?

                        WIFE
        Because I think you're cute.

She pats his cheek. Leaving a smear of applesauce on it
as she leans over the baby with a bowl, to give her a
spoonful.

                        BABY
        WHHHAAAAA!!!!

                        WIFE
        You are too, precious wittle-muffie-puffie.

                        BABY
        WHHHAAAAA!!!!

Baby smacks away her mommy's hand, sending the spoon and
bowl flying. Applesauce splatters all over the wall and
floor.

                        BABY
        WHHHHAAAA!!!!

Wife smiles with determined delight.

                        WIFE
            (ever sweet)
        Such a good right hook!

Glaring at her husband, her smile crumbles into an
exhausted frown.

                        WIFE
        There's a case in the garage.

                        BABY
        WHHHAAAA!!!!

On dazed autopilot, she plods out of the kitchen. The
baby stops crying. Keeps her tiny voice low, yet urgent.

                    BABY
          Before she gets back. Quick! Two of us need
          to huddle.

                    SCREENWRITER
          When did you start—?

                    BABY
              (cutting him off)
          Really think, for even a freakin' moment, she
          can be objective?

                    SCREENWRITER
          Kind of hoped.

                    BABY
          She's too close to you, pop.

                    SCREENWRITER
          Because she's my wife?

                    BABY
          And mother of me, for crying out loud, your
          darling little bundle of joy!

Screenwriter rubs his chin again. A moment of
introspection.

                    BABY
          Don't start fretting. Rehearsing with a
          loved one's fine, especially for getting
          comfortable with your words. But comfy, pop,
          ain't gonna land you that three picture deal.
          And it sure as heck won't pay back those
          student loans.

                    SCREENWRITER
              (suddenly troubled)
          Pay back . . . ?

                    BABY
          Find someone experienced, who'll be brutally
          honest yet constructive.

                    SCREENWRITER
          Student loans . . . ?

Hearing footsteps, BABY motions to his lip-quivering
father.

                    BABY
     Shhh! Act normal!

Wife strides back into the kitchen, jar in hand. Again
sweet as can be.

                    WIFE
     I've got apple-saucy.

                    SCREENWRITER
          (losing it)
     WHHHHAAAA!!!!

Bewildered, Wife glances at the Baby. The little one
shrugs.

EXT. BACK YARD — DAY

Sunlight streams through the leaves of a billowing oak.
His composure regained, Screenwriter pumps his fist
triumphantly.

                    SCREENWRITER
     . . . It rips! Virgil plummets to his death,
     twenty stories below.

He smiles. Lowers his fist. Waits. And waits.

                    SCREENWRITER
     What do you think? Any reaction to the
     pitch, either way?
          (smile fading)
     Come on, buddy. Be truthful. Yea or nay,
     thumb's up or thumb's down?

Sitting on the grass, his droll, droopy-eyed HOUND
drones.

                    HOUND
     I don't have thumbs, dim-wad, I've got paws.
     I'm a dog.

                    SCREENWRITER
          (cringing)
     And I thought I could count on you for
     helpful suggestions.

                    HOUND
     What I'm trying to say is, know who you're
     pitching. Do your homework. Don't bring a
     thriller to a company that only makes
     comedies . . .

SCREENWRITER
Because they'd be predisposed to say no.

HOUND
You'd be barking up the wrong tree. And
people resent having their time wasted.

Screenwriter chuckles.

SCREENWRITER
Guess it's a dog-eat-dog world out there,
isn't it?

HOUND
(scowling)
I fail to see the humor.

SCREENWRITER
Sorry. Any other advice, would be greatly
appreciated.

HOUND
There are some things you should do to get
ready.

Lifting one of his hind legs, the dog begins to lick
himself.

HOUND
(muttering)
Mmmm . . . It's good to be canine.

SCREENWRITER
That's what I should do?

Hound stops licking.

HOUND
Don't be absurd.
(rolls his drooping eyes)
Okay, in terms of story, figure out everything
you possibly can about your characters and
the world they function in.

SCREENWRITER
Obviously. In case questions about them come
up in the meeting.

HOUND
But to get to the questions, you've first got
to grab their attention.

SCREENWRITER
So . . . ? I should prepare . . . ?

                         HOUND
Three variations. Start with the elevator
pitch. One slam-dunk, on-the-nose statement
that drives the story home. Some call it the
bomb. Between floors you realize, oh my gosh,
that's no bellhop standing next to me. It's
Warner Sony Fox. Got time for one line to
blow him away, get him wanting to know more.

                     SCREENWRITER
Try one on me. Going up . . .

Screenwriter pushes an imagery elevator button.

                     SCREENWRITER
Ding. 2nd floor.

                         HOUND
Romeo and Juliet on a sinking ship.

                     SCREENWRITER
Ding, 3rd floor, tell me more.

                         HOUND
''Titanic.''

Screenwriter smiles in realization.

                     SCREENWRITER
What's next?

                         HOUND
The short pitch. Super tight. Three
sentences, in the present tense. Nailing
character, conflict, and genre. Structured
beginning, middle, and end.

                     SCREENWRITER
Let me give it a shot.

Screenwriter clears his throat.

                     SCREENWRITER
Exploring dysfunctional separation in the
modern nuclear family—

                         HOUND
Stop! You're in the doghouse already! Don't
pitch theme. Pitch image, action.

                     SCREENWRITER
Then help me out. I was trying to do ''Mrs.
Doubtfire.''

Hound turns his shabby head the other way. Playing hard-
to-get.

Screenwriter sighs, tosses him a biscuit.

                    HOUND
          (chewing)
     Yummm. Mmmmmm. Good to be canine.
          (swallowing)
     Okay. Like this: Slacker voice-over artist
     is kicked out by his wife. Disguises himself
     as a Scottish Nanny to remain close to the
     kids. Cleans up his own life by cleaning up
     theirs.

Screenwriter chuckles.

                    HOUND
     See, made you laugh, didn't I? You even got
     that it's a comedy.

                    SCREENWRITER
     And for the third variation?

                    HOUND
     You get their attention, be ready to deliver
     the full pitch. Keep it concise, no more
     than ten minutes long. These are busy
     people, ADD's an occupational hazard. Sell
     the sizzle, avoid rambling details. Stay
     with pivotal scenes, keep it visual. Know
     your target audience, and stay focused, on
     track.

                    SCREENWRITER
     Zeroed in like a laser beam! On HDTV!

                    HOUND
     Be psychologically ready to handle each and
     every distraction. A nine-point quake hits
     and you're in the midst of your pitch, finish
     it when you climb out of the rubble.

                    SCREENWRITER
     One shot to get it right. Right?

                    HOUND
     Score a bull's eye. Or come away with
     nothing.

Screenwriter scratches himself behind his ear.

                    SCREENWRITER
     Wow. Anything else?

                    HOUND
        Arrive early. Be prepared to wait. And turn
        off your cell phone!

Hound licks himself again. Contemplative, Screenwriter
chews on one of the dog biscuits.

INT. PRODUCER'S OFFICE — DAY

Unattended, oversized desk. Open-shuttered window with
a partial backlot view. Paneled walls crowded with
photographs of glad-handing celebs and politicos. Three
sofas arranged for focal conversation.

Sitting on one, a typed synopsis of his pitch in hand,
the Screenwriter. Across from him, unlit cigar clenched
in his glaring white teeth, the tight-skinned PRODUCER
sports a not-too-convincing toupee. D-GUY, a youthful
development exec, sits on the third. Aggressively
affecting a casual demeanor.

                    PRODUCER
        So what've you got?

Screenwriter leans forward. To take control of the
room.

                    SCREENWRITER
        A struggling screenwriter goes to Hell—

                    PRODUCER
              (cutting him off)
        You say a screenwriter?

Producer leans forward. To take control of the room.

                    SCREENWRITER
        That's right.

                    PRODUCER
        Goes to Hell?

                    SCREENWRITER
        Correct.

Producer glances at D-Guy. D-Guy almost squirms.
Uncertain if he's being brought into the conversation.

Producer mulls. Chews on his cigar. Following his lead,
D-Guy ponders, as well.

                    PRODUCER
     Toxic gasses, fiery abyss. A spiny pathway to
     eternal condemnation . . .

Producer arches a brow.

                    PRODUCER
     I like it.

                    D-GUY
          (jumping in)
     Good so far.

                    PRODUCER
     Screenwriter goes to Hell. Exactly where he
     belongs!

                    D-GUY
     I've always thought so!

Producer gives Screenwriter a sly look. Taking him into
his confidence.

                    PRODUCER
     Give me the gist of it.

                    SCREENWRITER
     A struggling screenwriter goes to Hell, to
     learn how to write a great screenplay so he
     can impress a hot actress.

                    PRODUCER
     Hot actress . . . Starlet type, maybe an
     ingénue?

Screenwriter nods. Producer mulls. D-Guy ponders.

                    PRODUCER
     Curvaceous? Not-too-bright?

                    SCREENWRITER
     Let's just say, a lot smarter than she lets
     on.

                    PRODUCER
          (knowingly)
     Beautiful.

                    D-GUY
     Great concept!

                    PRODUCER
          Reminds me.

Producer presses a button on the intercom by the couch.

                    PRODUCER
          Marge, call Ashley. Tell her meet me, eight
          on-the-dot, wear that low-cut scarlet clingy
          thing.

                    MARGE
               (over intercom)
          Will do.

Producer rolls the cigar in his pearly whites.

                    PRODUCER
          Okay, all right, lay a little more on me.
          This screenwriter . . . ?

                    SCREENWRITER
          Danny. Wants to score with Bebe, who leads
          him on, but tells him first, he has to write
          her a great script.

                    PRODUCER
          Been there.

                    D-GUY
          Done that!

                    SCREENWRITER
          . . . He meets mysterious Virgil, a more
          seasoned writer who offers to show him the
          way, but reminds him that sometimes, to get
          to paradise, you've got to go through a
          little hell . . .

Producer pushes the button on the intercom.

                    PRODUCER
          Marge, call my wife. Tell her I'm swamped.
          Won't be home for dinner, don't wait up.

                    MARGE
               (over intercom)
          If she asks what you're doing?

                    PRODUCER
               (irritated)
          I don't know. You want to work in movies?
          Make up a story!

Producer returns his attention to the Screenwriter.

14.

                    PRODUCER
Temps.

                    SCREENWRITER
. . . So, battling bloodthirsty demons of the
netherworld, Danny learns what it takes to be
a screenwriter.

Producer scratches his head, adjusts his toupee.   Gives
D-Guy a look.

                    PRODUCER
Raises some questions, doesn't it?

                    D-GUY
Certainly does.

Producer glares at him.

                    D-GUY
Oh, uh, why does Danny, if he's already a
screenwriter, need this guy Virgil to show
him the ropes? And why does Virgil need him?

                    PRODUCER
Because it's obvious why they both need the
actress.
          (winking knowingly)
He, he . . .

Producer snickers.   Chews on his unlit cigar.   D-Guy
titters.

                    D-GUY
He, he . . .

                    SCREENWRITER
Beyond his relative inexperience, Danny's big
on creativity, but low on craft. Virgil, on
the other hand, has craft down pat. But his
imagination's gone completely out the window.

                    PRODUCER
Boy, do we know writers like that.

                    D-GUY
Boy, do we!

                    SCREENWRITER
I'm calling it, ''Screenwriting for the Hell
of It.'' It's a very loose adaptation . . .
well, parody actually, of Dante's
''Inferno . . .''

The Producer is taken aback. Shoots D-Guy another look.
The pitch unexpectedly seems to grind to a halt.

                    PRODUCER
          Do we know Dante?

                    D-GUY
          Didn't he direct ''Gremlins?''

                    SCREENWRITER
          No, you're thinking of Joe—

                    PRODUCER
          We should get some coverage on this
          ''Inferno.'' Check on the rights.

                    D-GUY
          I'll call the guild, track down his agent.

                    SCREENWRITER
          It's been in the public domain for quite a
          while now.

Producer lets out a tense breath. Screenwriter's got
all the answers.

                    PRODUCER
          Ah.
               (concerned)
          Oh. Not too old-hat, is it? Give me the
          whole tortilla.

D-Guy discreetly leans close to Producer.

                    D-GUY
               (whispering)
          I think you mean enchilada.

Producer glares at him. D-Guy cowers, sits back. Minds
his place.

Screenwriter tries to act like he hasn't noticed.

                    SCREENWRITER
          Penthouse. Champagne, candlelight. Danny's
          putting the make on starlet Bebe, hot and
          heavy. She gives him the stiff arm, tells
          him, ''You wanna get to third base, write me
          a great screenplay . . .''

Producer takes out his BlackBerry. Scrolls down to
check on something. Screenwriter keeps pitching.

SCREENWRITER
Danny's insecure, doesn't know if he's got it
in him. So he goes to Timber's Tavern and
throws a drunk. Virgil, seemingly out of the
blue, appears next to him on a stool . . .

Producer smirks. Focused on BlackBerry, he keys in a
note.

SCREENWRITER
Tells him, he can show him how to—

PRODUCER
(without glancing up)
Who's the audience?

The question is so abrupt, Screenwriter's almost thrown.
But he stays on his game.

SCREENWRITER
Just about anybody and everybody who's ever
wanted to learn how to write a screenplay.
Picture Hades, where each level demonstrates
a different element of screenwriting.

PRODUCER
Hmmmmm.

Producer puts away the BlackBerry. Narrows a glance
toward D-Guy.

D-GUY
Hmmmmm.

PRODUCER
You thinking what I'm thinking?

D-GUY
With you one hundred percent.

Producer pauses. Gives him the floor. D-Guy suddenly
looks pained. Not really knowing what they're thinking.

Producer groans.

PRODUCER
(to Screenwriter)
I go with my gut. Doesn't really sound like
a movie.

Screenwriter deflates.

> PRODUCER
> But it just might be a manual.

He pushes the button on the intercom.

> PRODUCER
> Marge, get my good friend David Barker on the speakerphone. He's at Continuum International.

Smiles at the Screenwriter.

> PRODUCER
> I want him to hear this. You've got to know your market, kid. Got to go where it flows.

Screenwriter hesitates, uncertain.

D-Guy gives him a subtle, reassuring nod.

Screenwriter digests the thought. And returns their smiles.

FADE TO BLACK

"SCREENWRITING FOR THE HELL OF IT"

by

Mark Evan Schwartz

Log Line

A loose parody of Dante's *Inferno*, in which struggling writer Danny, need-ing to learn how to write a great screenplay so he can score with a hot actress, is guided by mysterious Virgil through the netherworld, where each level of Hades represents a different element of screenwriting.

Synopsis

ACT ONE

Wanting to score with starlet Bebe, Danny is told that if he wants to get anywhere with her he's going to have to write her a great screenplay. Unbeknownst to Danny, someone is lurking, listening, in the shadows. With a draft of his screenplay in hand, Danny feels he might have the talent, but frets he lacks the craft. He goes drinking at Timber's Tavern. Seasoned screenwriter Virgil mysteriously appears on the stool next to him, and assures him he can show him how to write a great screenplay. "But to get to paradise," Virgil informs him, "sometimes you have to go through a little hell." So begins a journey through Hades, where each level represents a different element of screenwriting. Guided by Virgil, Danny's first lesson is about structure. They watch examples from movies on fiery canyon walls. Convinced that he now knows everything he's supposed to, Danny dashes back to tell Bebe. He's surprised to discover her entertaining someone else.

ACT TWO

Danny, moping back to the tavern, crosses paths again with Virgil and admits he has a lot to learn about character. Returning to the netherworld with his screenplay, Virgil takes Danny to a hellish nightclub to show him the essentials of character. Danny witnesses ghoulish behavior that shows him how character is defined cinematically, and he sees what distinguishes the protagonist from the antagonist, as well as the functions of the various supporting characters that surround them. Taking him to a library of the dead, Virgil goes on to show Danny how to create characters so they will come to life on the page. Confident that he's resolved all his issues related to screenwriting, Danny again returns to the material world and Bebe. She's once more unimpressed, telling him his script still doesn't work. Danny sulks back to Timber's, fretting he should just give up. Virgil again magically appears and, more evasive then ever about his own true motives, convinces Danny he can still show him other elements he needs to learn. Heading back to hell, Virgil exposes Danny to the functions of dialogue, with two condemned actors playing out scenes that make what they say cinematic. Once there, beginning to see how structure, character, dialogue, and action all fit together, Danny is taken to yet another level where, in the innards of a ghastly beast, Virgil shows him what constitutes a scene. Pursued by monsters, he experiences how it all propels plotting. Escaping, subplots are also defined. And arriving at a giant, monolithic script, Virgil gives Danny the specifics of format. Positive now that he knows what he needs to craft his screenplay, Danny is unexpectedly clobbered by Virgil, who flees with Danny's script.

ACT THREE

Shaking off Virgil's assault, Danny takes off in pursuit. Meanwhile, Virgil is with Bebe. He's got the script, which Danny has not copyrighted or registered. Furthermore, Danny is completely without representation. So Virgil reveals he intends to put his name on it; no one will be the wiser. As Bebe begins to protest, Danny returns to throttle Virgil's plan. Trying to turn things in his favor, Virgil convinces him the script needs a rewrite and, detailing what to look for and how to consider revisions, tries to talk him into letting him do it. Danny refuses. Bebe, torn in her allegiance, recognizing Virgil's craft and Danny's talent, proposes collaboration. A climatic tug-of-war over the script leads to the rooftop, with Bebe stuck in the middle as the two men fight to get the upper hand, and one of them plummets to his death.

Character Profiles

1. Character's Name: Daniel Cardigan
2. Nickname: Danny
3. Gender: Male
4. Age: 27
5. Physical Appearance: Boyish, slight build
6. Occupation: Struggling screenwriter
7. Marital / Romantic Status: Single, on the make
8. Sexual Orientation: Heterosexual
9. Friend(s): A couple writing buddies
10. Place of Birth: Omaha, Nebraska
11. Places Lived: Nebraska and L.A.
12. Parents: Julie, elementary school teacher, and Robert, engineer. Still married
13. Siblings: Missy, still in college, and Robert Jr., pediatrician
14. Education: M.A. English. University of Nebraska
15. Religion: Methodist
16. Ethnicity: Caucasian
17. Socio-Economic Status: Broke. Still living like a Grad Student
18. Politics: Liberal Democrat
19. Tastes in Music: Eclectic and alternative rock
20. Tastes in Movies, Theater, TV: Passionate about all genres of film, theater, and anthology television. Hates reality TV
21. Tastes in Clothes: Cargoes, flannel shirts, casual
22. Favorite Foods and Drink: Fast foods, beer and tequila
23. Hobbies: Spends all his spare time writing, going to the movies
24. Talents and Skills: Storytelling, drawing. No known outside skills
25. Personality Traits: Likable, easy going, good humored, gullible
26. Psychological Traits: Insecurity and self-doubt

MISSION

Greatest Need: To achieve self-value through quality work
Motivation: Lust for a beautiful actress
Defining Activity: Willingness to go to Hell and back

OBSTACLE

Greatest Weakness: Deep insecurity. Big on talent, small on craft
Problem It Creates: Inability to make progress on writing
Defining Activity: Getting drunk instead of writing

1. Character's Name: V. Goldman Towne
2. Nickname: Virgil
3. Gender: Male
4. Age: Late 40s
5. Physical Appearance: Middle-aged bohemian
6. Occupation: Screenwriter
7. Marital / Romantic Status: Single. Twice divorced
8. Sexual Orientation: Heterosexual
9. Friends: Anyone he thinks can advance his career
10. Place of Birth: Los Angeles
11. Places Lived: Only L.A.
12. Parents: Marjorie, realtor, and Harve, personal injury attorney. Divorced when Virgil was 5
13. Siblings: None
14. Education: Film school drop out
15. Religion: Half Jewish, half Catholic
16. Ethnicity: Caucasian
17. Socio-Economic Status: Made a lot of money, lost a lot of money. Repeatedly
18. Politics: Left of center
19. Tastes in Music: 60s rock
20. Tastes in Movies, Theater, TV: All popular studio genres. Rarely goes to theater
21. Tastes in Clothes: Denim pants, cotton shirts, sports coats
22. Favorite Food and Drink: California cuisine, Bloody Marys
23. Hobbies: Gambling
24. Talents and Skills: Writing, tennis
25. Personality Traits: Persistent, manipulative, deceitful
26. Psychological Traits: Inflated ego masking fears of failure

MISSION

Greatest Need: To achieve self-value through financial success
Motivation: Commitment of a marketable actress
Defining Activity: Manipulating the confidence of a naïve young writer

OBSTACLE

Greatest Weakness: Self-absorption. Big on craft, small on talent
Problem It Creates: Blindness to people's true needs
Defining Activity: Convincing young writer to go with him to Hell

1. Character's Name: Barbara La Rue
2. Nickname: Bebe
3. Gender: Female
4. Age: Mid-thirties, but pretends to be younger
5. Physical Appearance: Voluptuous
6. Occupation: Movie star
7. Marital / Romantic Status: Single. Available to the right people
8. Sexual Orientation: Heterosexual, but open to experimentation
9. Friends: Her hairdresser, manicurist, personal trainer, and plastic surgeon
10. Place of Birth: Baton Rouge, Louisiana
11. Places Lived: New York, Los Angeles
12. Parents: Peggy May, housewife, Joe Don, carpet salesman and part time minister
13. Siblings: Three older brothers that work at their father's store
14. Education: Acting classes, New York and L.A.
15. Religion: Pentecostal, but tells people she's agnostic
16. Ethnicity: Caucasian, with traces of Cajun
17. Socio-Economic Status: Upper middle-class
18. Politics: Apolitical, unless advised otherwise by her manager
19. Tastes in Music: Show tunes, jazz, standards
20. Tastes in Movies, Theater, TV: Whatever is in vogue
21. Tastes in Clothes: Clingy and revealing
22. Favorite Foods and Drink: Veggies, champagne
23. Hobbies: Collecting movie memorabilia
24. Talents and Skills: Acting, manipulation
25. Personality Traits: Sexy, sensual, alternatingly coy and direct, driven
26. Psychological Traits: Narcissistic

MISSION:

Greatest Need: To be loved forever as a star of the silver screen
Motivation: Stars need great scripts to shine in
Defining Activity: Manipulating a naïve young writer

OBSTACLE

Greatest Weakness: Self-absorption. All gloss and no depth
Problem It Creates: Blindness to the emotional impact she has on others
Defining Activity: Convincing young writer she'll be his if he writes her a great script

Beat Outline

ACT ONE:

Set Up: Bebe's penthouse apartment. Danny puts the make on her. She tells him if he wants to score to write her a great screenplay.

Inciting Incident: Dejected Danny gets drunk. Meets mysterious Virgil in bar. Virgil tells him he can show him how to write (craft) a great screenplay. Protag's mission is defined. Virgil: "But to get to paradise, sometimes you have to go through a little hell."

Danny arrives in Hades with Virgil. Crossing the fiery River Styx, he learns the basic differences of storytelling in novels, plays, and movies.

On a battlefield, Danny witnesses a struggle between character and structure. Virgil tells him these writers are condemned because they never learned that the two go hand-in-hand.

A cryptic canyon. Virgil begins by telling Danny about classic three-act structure.

"Telling" is too abstract. So Virgil "cinematically shows" him. Scenes from *Tootsie* and *Gladiator* are projected on a canyon wall. Compared structurally.

Danny decides he knows all he needs to know. Virgil tries to stop him as he dashes back to the material world, and Bebe.

He finds that Bebe is "entertaining" somebody else.

Further dejected, Danny goes back to bar. Meets up with Virgil. Acknowledges he still has a lot to learn, especially about character.

ACT TWO:

Returning to uptown Hades. Virgil tells Danny function of protagonist and antagonist. Still too abstract. So Virgil takes him to a nightclub to show him.

In Nightclub of the Dead with Virgil, Danny watches condemned, interacting singles deal with a variety of obstacles. Sees how character in movies is defined. Meanwhile, Virgil is becoming more evasive.

At Nether World Library, Danny learns from Virgil how to create those characters.

Strolling through streets of fire, Danny learns various functions of supporting characters.

Danny suddenly awakens at Bebe's. She's read his script. She hates it, thinks its boring, the dialogue's bad, the format's way off.

Midpoint: Back at the bar, Danny wallows in self-pity. Frets he'll never be able to write a great screenplay. Virgil appears again. Virgil uses Danny's anger to segue into dialogue.

A bizarre vehicle, "flying" back to hell. Danny has his screenplay. Virgil explains how dialogue works. Again, it's abstract. So via in-flight movies, hologram actors Rock and Doris show Danny.

Inner earth: Gobbled up by a monster. Danny and Virgil are trapped in its belly. Danny: what will happen next!? Virgil defines plotting. Unbeknownst to them, ingested freaks are in pursuit.

They escape. Trek toward distant monolith. Virgil teaches Danny about subplots.

Monolith is revealed to be giant bound screenplay. Virgil instructs Danny on standard screenplay format.

Danny, script in hand, feels he's got the basics of craft. Bebe calls, asking Virgil if he made an agreement with Danny. Evasive, Virgil lies to Danny about the call. Clobbers him, knocks him out. Steals his script. Danny didn't see it coming.

ACT THREE:

Danny comes to. Struggles back to material world.

Bebe's penthouse. Virgil tells her Danny didn't register or copyright script, and he has no representation. Explains how to do it. Then reveals he's going to steal it, rewrite it to make it his own.

Danny bursts in. Tension mounts with Virgil. Bebe suggests they do a rewrite together (Danny's talent, Virgil's craft). Discuss how to objectively approach it.

Climax: Tension explodes between Danny and Virgil. Rooftop tug of war over script. Bebe stuck in the middle. Script tears in half. Virgil falls.

Danny startles awake at his computer. His girlfriend beckons him to bed. Was it all just a dream?

Treatment

ACT ONE

Penthouse living room. Candlelight. Boyish DANNY, 27, is coming on to BEBE, hot and heavy. He's a struggling writer. She's a sexy actress. She tells him if he wants to get anywhere with her, he's going to have to write her a great screenplay. Glancing over Danny's shoulder, unseen by him, she subtly acknowledges the mysterious presence of SOMEONE peering out from the shadows of her bedroom.

Dejected, Danny's drinking his woes away in Timber's Tavern. Referring to the script he brought with him, he's just not sure if he's got it in him to write a great one. A voice startles him, VIRGIL seemingly appears out of nowhere. He baits Danny with his insider's knowledge of issues relating to screenwriting, and leaves the bar. Danny chases him down, taking the bait.

Cornering Virgil near an alley, Danny asks him if he can teach him how to write a great screenplay. An odd glimmer begins to radiate nearby. Virgil responds that while he can't teach him to be talented, he can certainly teach him how to use the craft. Danny is game. Virgil tells him it won't be easy, as the glimmer in the nearby alley intensifies. Because to get to paradise, Virgil coaxes, sometimes you have to go through a little hell. With screenplay in hand, Danny follows him into the glimmer. Disappearing through the portal.

On a smoldering beach on the edge of eternity, Danny gets his first glimpse of bad screenwriters, condemned to life in hell. Shaken, clutching his screenplay close, Danny asks Virgil how long he is going to have to stay here. Virgil tells him the choice is his. It's all a matter of how much he wants to learn.

Virgil approaches a PILOT, and asks him to row them to the other side. Crossing the fiery waters, the grumpy pilot butts in as Virgil tries to tell

Danny what the basic storytelling differences are between narrative film, theater, and books. Novels are about "what people think." Plays, "what people say." And movies, Danny learns, are about "what people do." Losing control, the pilot falls overboard. Burning up in the gurgling water.

A battle rages on the beachhead on other side. Battered souls at odds, duking it out, structure versus character. Virgil tells Danny that's why they are doomed, because they haven't figured out that structure and character must go hand-in-hand.

Moving on, they come upon a huge, incandescent road map mounted between the walls of a cryptic canyon. It charts fifteen primary plot points of classic three-act structure: Set Up, Inciting Incident, Protagonist Decision, Antagonist Reaction, End of Act One/Reversal, New Direction, Decisions, Reactions, Midpoint, Protagonist Decision, Antagonist Reaction, End of Act Two/Reversal, Colliding Courses of Action, Climax, Resolution/Ending Act Three. Totally abstract. Without supporting images and actions, Danny is thoroughly confused, even a little bored. So Virgil magically parts the map for Danny and reveals a gigantic shimmering movie screen.

As an AUDIENCE OF GHOULS gathers to watch, corn popping over hell's fires, Virgil shows a double feature: *Gladiator* and *Tootsie*. Cutting to different scenes, Danny sees how, in spite of their differences in genre, setting, scope, and tone, the two movies utilize the identical three-act structure, and how it fits in with the arc of its leading characters. As Danny's enthusiasm grows, so does the crowd's, shouting for Virgil and him to shut up. Their talk is spoiling the movies.

Excited, Danny proclaims he's got to tell Bebe what he's learned. Virgil tries to stop him, because they've barely scratched the surface on character. Reminding Virgil he can leave anytime, Danny dashes back to the material world. Virgil's concerned.

Danny arrives at Bebe's penthouse, practically bursting at the seams. But he discovers she's not alone. Someone else's screenplay is on her coffee table, along with an open bottle of champagne. A mysterious presence closes her bedroom door. Crushed, Danny leaves. He just didn't see it coming.

Nearing the tavern, he crosses paths with Virgil, who's waiting for him at the alleyway. Acknowledging that he has got a lot to learn about character, script still in hand, Danny follows Virgil back through the portal.

ACT TWO

Date night. Uptown Hades. Outside Brimstone's, Virgil tells Danny about the functions of the leading characters. The protagonist's mission, his or her goals, are what the story is about. The antagonist creates obstacles, generating conflict. Giving the story its sense of drama. Elbowing to the front of a LINE OF HIDEOUS CREEPS, whispering a bribe to the BOUNCER, Virgil takes Danny inside. Danny wants to know what Virgil said. But Virgil is increasingly evasive about his own motivations and methods.

Brimstone's. A necro-rave is raging. GHOULISH HUNKS hit on GIRLIE GHOULETTES at the bar and on the dance floor. They're clearly getting turned down, cold dead, even though the throbbing music drowns out their words. Knocking back a Bloody Mary, Virgil and Danny can see the various ways the hunks are reacting to the brush-offs, and Virgil uses it to illustrate how character is defined in cinematic stories. "Decisive action taken when confronted by obstacle." Seeing actions "speaking louder than words," Danny finds he understands a great deal about whom these characters are, even without being able to hear what they're saying. He refers to his own script, and takes careful notes, declaring Bebe would love to play some of the actions and reactions that he's witnessing. Now if only he could figure out what Virgil's really up to? Virgil again evades, telling him how protagonists must show a full range of human traits, so the audience can relate to them. And while the best ones are fully fleshed out, antagonists don't necessarily have to be human at all. Suddenly the GREAT WHITE SHARK from *Jaws* rips through the floor, startling the piss out of Danny.

In the bathroom, Danny washes up while Virgil defines fundamental differences between a character's objectives from scene to scene, and his or her mission throughout the course of a story. As in *Die Hard*, the protagonist's objective in a given scene might be to kill one of the thieves, but his overall mission is to reconcile with his estranged wife. Danny asks what tools Virgil suggests he use to create such characters?

Netherworld Public Library. Surrounded by DEMONS, dust, and decay, Virgil whispers to Danny about the benefits of coupling research with imagination. In the community room, he shows him a character profile "laundry list," reminding him the more you know your characters, the better you'll be able to build a story around them, and the obstacles needed to define them. A DECREPIT DEAD GUY with a bloody pencil jammed in his forehead raises his withered hand: "Anything else to clue-in the audience?"

Strolling back through the pre-dawn town, Virgil goes over with Danny various functions of supporting characters. They can help the audience better know the protagonist or antagonist, provide insights and exposition, and perform actions that advance plot and illustrate theme. He gives examples from great movies ranging from *Star Wars* to *Platoon* and *Schindler's List*. Thoughtfully glancing toward the rising fiery orb, Virgil asks Danny what he's thinking?

Bebe's voice, and a table lamp, wakes Danny in her penthouse living room. He'd fallen asleep on her couch. She tells him she's read his screenplay. He perks up, wants to know what she thinks. She tells him the structure is sound, the characters are beginning to take shape, but over all it "blew the big one." Danny is crushed. Bebe tells him the scenes lack "oomph," his dialogue's "dribble," and the format is so off base, it's not even in the ballpark.

Crestfallen, Danny returns to Timber's Tavern, resigned to his fears that he will never be worth a damn as a screenwriter. Virgil again appears, startling him. He tells Danny he's just reached his "midpoint," and observes how being there is connected with his "inciting incident." Danny's indignant, refusing to believe that his life is a screenplay. Virgil convinces him to step outside.

They climb into a hovering Nethercraft Sports Coup and blast-downward-off, descending back toward the netherworld. Virgil engages Danny in a dialogue about dialogue, how it functions cinematically, even visually, to advance character, relationship, plot, and above all else, dramatic conflict. Illustrating how it differs from the potentially mundane way people speak in real life, Virgil projects contrasting scenes from in-flight movies, enacted by holograms ROCK and DORIS. Meanwhile, glimpsed through the Nethercraft's porthole, a GARGANTUAN WINGED SLUG slogs through the inner-earth's atmosphere, gaining in size and momentum, getting closer and closer. Danny shouts out . . . just as the slug swallows them up.

Which brings Virgil to the topic of plot, how its function is to keep the viewer involved from scene to scene, by making them always want to know what's going to happen next. They climb out of the wrecked craft, into the gooey digestive fluids of the slug's stomach. As they slosh their way through it, Danny being careful not to get his script wet, Virgil defines what constitutes a scene, and how story devices like cliffhangers and unanswered questions help keep audiences engaged. Behind them, INGESTED PSYCHOTIC FREAKS begin stalking. Another device, Virgil muses, is the hidden reveal. Suddenly the freaks lunge, snarling that they want Danny's screenplay. The two flee for their lives.

Narrowly escaping through the slug's esophagus, they're belched like projectiles from its gaping mouth and clump to the ground, tumbling through a scarlet field of incandescent grass. Danny's grateful his screenplay is undamaged. Questioned again about his own motives, Virgil once more evasively switches subjects, this time to subplots. Trekking toward a White Rectangular Monolith, he uses the thematically linked subplots from *Die Hard* as examples. Having received so much valuable craft information, increasingly weary from his journey, Danny asks what else he could possibly need to know.

At the monolith, revealed to be a towering bound screenplay, Virgil answers: "Standard Screenplay Format." After all this hard work, Virgil informs him, no producer, director, development exec, story editor, or analyst will bother reading his script if doesn't look right on the page. He explains why format has evolved the way it has, and then gives him all the specifics. Danny sets his screenplay on the ground, so he can help Virgil turn the pages of the monolithic script to see examples. Virgil's cell phone rings. Bebe, wanting to know what's up? Virgil covers, telling Danny it's just a solicitor. Then continues with his lesson. Closing the towering script, Danny says that he's satisfied now he's learned everything he needs to. "Not quite," Virgil responds. He suddenly pushes the monolith over, on top of Danny, splatting him under it like a flyswatter whacking a bug.

Picking Danny's screenplay up off the ground, Virgil smirks: "Didn't see it coming, Danny. Did you?" He vanishes through an unzipped crevice with Danny's script.

ACT THREE

Struggling out from under the monolithic screenplay with all his might, Danny manages to leap through the crevice just before it zips closed.

Squirming through to the other side, he finds himself in Bebe's boudoir. He is dismayed to hear her talking with Virgil in the living room. He creeps to the partially open bedroom door to listen.

Pleased with himself, Virgil smugly tells Bebe the kid never even bothered to get his first draft registered or copyrighted, and that he's totally without representation. So telling her how to go about it, he says he's going to steal Danny's screenplay by putting his name on it and declaring it his own. Danny rushes into the room, shouting, "When Hell freezes over!" Demanding that Virgil give him back his script, Danny whips out a gun. Seeing the unforeshadowed weapon as too conveniently easy, Bebe suggests compromise. Like this script, the one that they're in, Danny's needs a re-write, as all first drafts do. Perhaps, given Danny's creative talent and Virgil's grasp of craft, they could rewrite together and come up with a real winner. Hearing some approaches to rewriting, things that the writer can do to gain objectivity, Danny's defenses begin to weaken. But ruthless and desperate, Virgil grabs Bebe, threatening to paper-cut her throat with Danny's script if he doesn't back off.

Bebe in his clutches, Virgil backs onto the verandah, twenty stories high. Danny lunges! Stumbling, Virgil takes Bebe over the edge with him. Dangling, fearing for their lives, Virgil grips one end of the screenplay and Bebe, above him, the other, grabbing hold of Danny with her free hand. A climatic tableau straight out of *Die Hard*. The script rips in half. Virgil, screaming, plummets downward toward certain death as Danny, frantically pulling Bebe back up onto the verandah . . .

. . . startles awake. Dazed at his computer. Rubbing his weary eyes, clearing his head, he looks up at the poster of an old movie starring Bebe La Rue tacked on his wall. DANNY'S GIRLFRIEND, beckoning, asks him come to bed, suggesting he finish revisions tomorrow. Danny says in a few minutes, he's still grappling with his story's resolution. She tells him he knows where he can find her, if he needs a little inspiration. Rising, he's tempted. But he glances back at the page of script humming on his monitor.

FADE TO BLACK

SCREENWRITING FOR THE HELL OF IT

an original screenplay

by

Mark Evan Schwartz

Contact:

Mark Evan Schwartz
Loyola Marymount University
School of Film & Television
One LMU Drive
Los Angeles, CA 90045-2659

INT. BEBE'S PENTHOUSE LIVING ROOM — NIGHT

Seductive jazz on the stereo. Candlelight glistening
off a half finished bottle of champagne. Posed publicity
photos of a movie starlet crowd the mantle above a
crackling fire.

Cuddling on a sofa, DANNY, still boyish at 27, pulls
shapely BEBE LA RUE, the object of the photos, close for
a kiss. She resists. Breathy like a Hollywood goddess
from another era.

                    BEBE
          No, Danny. Not now. Not yet.

                    DANNY
          Come on, Bebe. I got this itch that's
          driving me crazy . . .

She smiles demurely. Danny takes it as a sign. He
slides his hand up her thigh, nibbles her ear.

                    DANNY
          And I need you to scratch it.

But she again pushes him away.

                    BEBE
          Know what I need?

Cocksure he's got the answer, he attempts another grope.

She suddenly stiff-arms him. Looks him straight in the
eye.

                    BEBE
          Structure.

                    DANNY
          Huh?

                    BEBE
          Coupled with character and a strong sense of
          mission.

                    DANNY
          I'm having a sense of mission.

He tries to mount her. She shoves him back.

                    BEBE
     But even that's not enough. I need more. So
     much more.
          (alluring)
     I need functional dialogue, Danny.
     Descriptive action, and resourceful
     plotting. And on top of it all, more than
     anything else, I need conflict. Obstacle.
     Dramatic tension.

He winces. Frustrated.

                    DANNY
     Oh, I've got tension all right.

                    BEBE
     Then wrap it in genre. And put it in format.

                    DANNY
     Bebe? What are we talking about?

                    BEBE
     Cinematic storytelling.

Bebe caresses his cheek. Beckons his eyes toward hers.

                    BEBE
     I'm an actress, Danny. And you're a
     wonderful, creative guy.

She provocatively pouts her lips.

                    BEBE
     Want to get to paradise? Write me a great
     screenplay.

She subtly glances over his shoulder, at her

BEDROOM DOOR

Slightly open. SOMEONE in the shadows peers out at them.

EXT. TIMBER'S PLACE — NIGHT

A dive off the warehouse district downtown. Broken red
neon crackles TIMBER'S P ACE above the always-open door.

INT. TIMBER'S PLACE — NIGHT

A gravelly Tom Waits love song mournfully plays on a
jukebox. Scattered DOWN AND OUTERS conspire over
pitchers of beer like nighthawks, or drown their sorrows
in cheap booze.

Danny perches alone on a wobbly stool at the bar.

                         DANNY
               (self-pitying)
          Supposed to come tripping out of my head and
          off of my fingers. Like magic. Easy-peazy.
          Nothing to it. Anybody can write a great
          script.

     The grizzled BARKEEP shakes his head in feigned empathy.
     He pours Danny another shot of tequila, and turns away to
     return the bottle to the mirrored shelf.

                         VIRGIL
               (abruptly)
          Apparently . . .

     Danny startles. A man out of nowhere sits beside him.

                         VIRGIL
          Just about everybody thinks they can. Sorry,
          friend. Didn't mean to rattle your pony.
               (knowingly)
          Thirty-five thousand.

     Casually studious in his jeans and sports coat, VIRGIL,
     late-40s cool, sips his draft beer.

                         DANNY
          Some sort of jackpot?

                         VIRGIL
          Hardly. The approximate number of properties
          registered every year at the Writer's Guild
          of America West.

                         DANNY
          Whoa.

                         VIRGIL
          Sobering, isn't it? Yeah. World's full of
          armchair screenwriters. Each and every
          inkslinging one of them convinced they've got
          a killer idea for a boffo movie. Know what?

     Danny shrugs. So does Virgil.

                         VIRGIL
          Maybe they do. Because ideas, man, they're
          around, practically for the asking. But
          finding a screenplay that works is like mining
          for gold.

     Virgil downs his draft. And winks.

                         VIRGIL
          Thanks for the brew.

He walks out of the bar.

Danny rubs his chin. Contemplative. He glances toward
the door.

                         DANNY
     Wait!

He tosses several bills on the counter, and chases after
him.

EXT. SIDEWALK NEAR ALLEY — NIGHT

Danny hurries out of the bar, past the red crackling
TIMBER'S P ACE neon. He catches up with Virgil near the
entrance to a shadowy alleyway.

                         DANNY
          Hold on a minute. Please . . .

Virgil pauses. Represses a smile.

                         DANNY
     Who are you?

                         VIRGIL
          Just another screenwriter, Danny.

                         DANNY
          (surprised)
     You know my name.

                         VIRGIL
     Omnipotence, bro. Lesson number one. The
     screenwriter has to know everything he
     possibly can about the universe of his
     screenplay, the folks that inhabit it.
     Otherwise, how can he make decisions that
     best serve the story? Choices, my man. What
     it ultimately comes down to.

He reaches out to shake hands.

                         VIRGIL
          V. Goldman Towne. Call me Virgil.

                         DANNY
          Okay, Virgil. Can you teach me how to write
     a great screenplay?

                    VIRGIL
     Tall freakin' order. I'm not going to lie to
     you, Danny-boy. Craft, you can learn. I can
     even show you some tools that'll help you use
     it. But great screenplays demand great
     stories. To write one of those requires an
     elusive little attribute called —

                    DANNY
     Talent.

A trace of insecurity crosses Danny's brow.

                    VIRGIL
     Creativity and imagination. If you got it, I
     can help you develop it.

                    DANNY
     Guess I'll never find out for sure, if I don't
     at least try.

                    VIRGIL
                (scrutinizing)
     Is she worth the effort?

Danny is surprised again. But then chuckles.

                    DANNY
     Do birds fly in the sky, fish swim in the sea?

                    VIRGIL
     Yeah. And bears crap in the woods, too.
     We'll work on your dialogue.

Amused, Virgil motions toward the dark alley. An
ethereal fog begins to swirl from a glimmer inside it.

Danny braces himself. Enters it with him.

EXT. SHADOWY ALLEY — NIGHT

They walk through shadows. The intensified glow looms
ahead.

                    VIRGIL
     Damned hard to write a great screenplay.
     Sometimes, man, to get to paradise, you've
     got to go through . . .

Danny hesitates. Virgil coaxes him on.

                    VIRGIL
     Well, you'll see.

They disappear in the swirling illumination.

EXT. NETHER BEACH — DAY

A fiery orb glares in the purple sky. Heat ripples from the yellow beach. Simmering crimson waves lap at the coastline that stretches past eternity.

Danny, with Virgil, gasps at what he sees. THOUSANDS OF DECREPIT, BAREFOOT MEN AND WOMEN frantically scream and yelp and holler in pain as they hop about on toe-scorching sand.

>   DANNY
>   Sinners?

>   VIRGIL
>   Bad screenwriters.

>   DANNY
>   How long will I have to be here?

>   VIRGIL
>   Totally up to you, Danny. Split anytime.
>   It's just a matter of how much you want to
>   learn.

They make their way to

A RICKETY ROWBOAT

Tied to the shore. Its ancient weathered PILOT waits moodily at the oars.

>   VIRGIL
>   Can you take us to the other side?

>   PILOT
>   (grumpy)
>   What do you think? I'm here to work on my
>   tan?

They climb in.

EXT. ROWBOAT — DAY

The pilot grunts, straining to row through crimson, steaming waters. Danny sweats profusely beside Virgil. Fiery spirals erupt around them.

>   DANNY
>   So much for all the naysayers, claiming
>   there's no such thing as global warming.

He shoots Danny as hostile look.

                    PILOT
Punk-ass upstart. Fancy you know so damn
much. Answer this: What are the fundamental
differences between writing film, theater, and
fiction?

                    DANNY
          (shrugging)
Writing's writing.

                    PILOT
Wrong, Mr. Smarty-pants! Wrong! Wrong! A
whole different mind-set applies. Novels,
for instance. Short stories, too. They're
about what people think!

                    VIRGIL
You see, fiction characteristically unfolds
introspectively, Danny. That's why it is
usually written in past tense. On reflection.

                    PILOT
          (annoyed)
Hey . . . !

                    VIRGIL
Fiction allows the reader to pause, reread,
and ponder.

                    PILOT
Ponder this: This is my scene! How come
you're doing so much yapping?

                    VIRGIL
Then tell him about theater.

                    PILOT
Plays!? Phooey! Talk, talk, talk!

                    VIRGIL
What he means, Danny, is that plays are
mostly about what people say. More than any
element, the dialogue is what communicates
the story.

                    PILOT
So the cheapskates in the back row, even if
they can't see the actors' itty-bitty little
expressions, will be able to follow what's
going on!

                    VIRGIL
Movies —

PILOT
Are about what people do! And I'll tell you
what I'm going to do!

Enraged, he leaps to his feet. The rowboat begins to
rock.

PILOT
If you don't mind your bee's wax and let me
have my say, I'm going to throw you the hell
off my boat!
(losing his balance)
Oops!

He tumbles overboard. A fiery splash.

Danny and Virgil watch the pilot burn up and go under.
Smoke whiffs in his wake.

VIRGIL
Yep. Movies are about what people do.

Virgil takes the oars, and starts to row.

EXT. ROCKY SHORE — DAY

Waves crash into jagged boulders at the bottom of
towering cliffs. Lightning streaks across the
turbulent, scarlet sky.

Virgil and Danny struggle against the tide as they
secure the rowboat to a petrified stump.

VIRGIL
Motion pictures, Danny. Sights and
sounds . . .

Percussive thunder rumbles.

EXT. SEASIDE CLIFF — DAY

Scaling a steep cliff, waves crashing far below, Danny
slips, nearly falls. Virgil extends his hand.

VIRGIL
. . . Stories unfolding through a series of
visual and aural reveals. Whipping past at
twenty-four frames per second. In the here
and now . . .

Danny grips Virgil's hand. Regains his footing.

                         VIRGIL
     . . . Which is why descriptive action in a
     screenplay should be concisely written, and
     must always be present tense . . .

Danny nods. They climb on.

EXT. TOP OF SEASIDE CLIFF — DAY

The wind howls. Lightning streaks, thunder booms.
Danny and Virgil hoist themselves to the top.

                         VIRGIL
     . . . Conforming as much as possible to the
     basic fundamentals I'm going to teach you.

                         DANNY
     Craft.

                         VIRGIL
     Like in any art form . . . whether it's
     painting abstracts, playing guitars, or
     weaving baskets . . . productive creativity
     grows out of a mastery of it. In writing
     movies, craft is essential. Because the goal
     in all screenwriting, no matter where your
     flights of fancy might take you, is one and
     the same.

                         DANNY
     To score with a hot actress?

                         VIRGIL
     To create a clear blueprint for a cinematic
     story! So the producer, director and actors,
     designers and technicians . . . So that
     everyone collaborating on making it will be
     able to communicate collectively to its
     intended audience.

                         DANNY
     Collaboration and communication.

                         VIRGIL
     It's at the heart of all narrative filmmaking.

Battle cries drift in with the wind.

                      BATTLE CRIES
                   (in the distance)
     Structure . . . ! Character . . . !

Danny looks toward the cries. Alarmed.

                         DANNY
          Then why are they fighting?

Turning his gaze with Danny's, Virgil sees

A DISTANT BATTLEFIELD

Armies of BATTERED SOULS repeatedly pound each other
like possessed slamdancers. Grotesquely OBESE GOBLINS
fiercely wallop deranged SKELETAL SPOOKS, viciously
whacking back.

                    SKELETAL SPOOKS
          Structure . . . !

                    OBESE GOBLINS
          Character . . . !

                         VIRGIL
                    (off screen)
          No wonder they're condemned.

ON THE CLIFF TOP

Danny glances at Virgil.

                         VIRGIL
          It's the screenwriting chicken or the egg,
          Danny. They're so hung up over which comes
          first, what best connects with a potential
          audience, they've lost sight that in movies
          structure and character go hand-in-hand.

                         DANNY
          You've lost me.

                         VIRGIL
          Come on. We've got to head in that
          direction, anyway.

He motions toward the battlefield.

Danny hesitates. Uneasy.

Virgil begins the trek, without looking back. Knowing
that he has no real choice, Danny follows.

EXT. BATTLEFIELD — DAY

Thunder rumbles through the lightning streaked clouds
above, barbarous slamdancing around them.

                    SKELETAL SPOOKS
          Structure . . . !

Spooks bang goblins. Skulls splinter. Virgil jerks
Danny out of harm's way.

                    VIRGIL
     . . . Is the way scenes in a movie are
     organized. How they interrelate.

                    OBESE GOBLINS
          Character . . . !

Goblins bash spooks. Torsos explode and spatter.
Virgil and Danny duck low.

                    DANNY
     . . . The people the movies are about.

                    VIRGIL
     Characters, yes. But character . . .
          (emphasizing)
     Character, Danny. Is about choice.

                    SKELETAL SPOOKS
          Structure!

Clobbering intensifies. Limbs snap, break off.

                    VIRGIL
     In American movies we traditionally use a
     three-act structure. Stories are
     communicated with a clear sense of beginning,
     middle, and end.

An Obese Goblin suddenly tries to block their way.

                    OBESE GOBLIN
          Character!

                    VIRGIL
     I'll cover specifics of that later, big fella.

Virgil fearlessly grabs Danny, and pushes past him.

They make their way off the battlefield, leaving
escalating violence behind.

EXT. CRYPTIC CANYON — DAY

Storm clouds still rumble. Fires burn on the eroded
walls of the canyon, the ground dry, barren, cracking.
Virgil and Danny trek on.

VIRGIL
Just keep in mind that in every dramatic
story there has to be both a protagonist and
an antagonist.

DANNY
The protagonist is the good guy.

VIRGIL
Usually. Think of it this way. It is the
protagonist's mission . . . the primary goal
or destination that he's trying to get to,
motivated by some deep-rooted need . . . that
drives the story. While the antagonist . . .

DANNY
The bad dude.

VIRGIL
Puts up most of the roadblocks . . . the
obstacles the protagonist must overcome . . .
to arrive at that goal. Their interaction is
what generates conflict. The very definition
of drama.
            (pausing)
As for structure, think of it as . . .

A gigantic, incandescent Road Map is mounted like a
crinkled dam looming between canyon walls.

VIRGIL
A map. With landmarks representing fifteen
primary plot points passed through during the
journey.

Fifteen points spark and burn on the map.

VIRGIL
Check 'em out: Set Up. Inciting Incident.
Decision. Reaction. End of Act One/
Reversal. New Direction. Decision.
Reaction. Midpoint. Another Decision. And
Reaction. End of Act Two/Reversal. New
Direction. Climax. Resolution ending Act
Three.

DANNY
What makes it special, if everyone is doing
it?

VIRGIL
The creativity you bring to it as a writer.
What the journey looks, sounds, and feels
            (MORE)

                    VIRGIL (cont'd)
like, the shape it takes, is dependant on
you.

Danny looks closer at the landmarks on the map.

                    DANNY
Tell me about the plot points, what they
mean.

                    VIRGIL
Act One. The Set Up establishes place,
period, and genre. Could be some
foreshadowing —

                    DANNY
Foreshadowing?

                    VIRGIL
An indication of some significant thing worth
paying attention to, that'll pay off later in
the story. There could even be the
suggestion of theme, what we're to gather
from the drama about the true nature of the
human spirit.

                    DANNY
And here I am, thinking movies are supposed
to be entertainment.

                    VIRGIL
Touch someone, Danny. They'll be
entertained.

The map scintillates, suddenly hotter.

                    VIRGIL
Act One continues with the Inciting Incident,
the event that literally jumpstarts the rest
of the story. An event that is so
meaningful, if it didn't happen, the story
might have gone in a different direction. Or
might not have happened at all.

                    DANNY
And it leads to —

                    VIRGIL
Decisions and Reactions being made, acted
upon by the protagonist and antagonist.
Steadily building to the unexpected event
triggering the End of Act One/Reversal.

                        DANNY
What do you mean?

                        VIRGIL
The protagonist appears en route to fulfilling
his mission. Something happens, usually
instigated by the antagonist, he doesn't
anticipate. It catches him by surprise,
propels him in a whole New Direction. "How
is he going to accomplish his mission now?"
the audience wonders. End of Act One.

Lightning suddenly strikes out of nowhere. Danny's
startled. More fires begin to burn.

                        DANNY
Uh . . . Act Two?

                        VIRGIL
The meat and potatoes of the story. The
longest act, where there's the most conflict.
The protagonist must make New Decisions. The
antagonist Reacts. Staring fate square in
the eye, the protagonist arrives at the
Midpoint.

                        DANNY
Defined as?

                        VIRGIL
A beat of false resolution, usually one of
two things. The protagonist feels he's found   .
what he's looking for, and accepts it. Or
fears he will never find it, and is resigned
to the cards dealt him.

Danny rubs his arms, feeling a spooky chill in spite of
the surrounding flames.

                        VIRGIL
But no. It's not over yet, sports fans. Act
Two continues. The protagonist makes New
Decisions leading to even stronger Reactions
from the antagonist. Surmounting those
obstacles, the protagonist is back on the
road to fulfilling his mission. But he is hit
again with something he doesn't see coming.

                        DANNY
End of Act Two/Reversal.

                        VIRGIL
Leaving the audience once again wondering,
"How is he going to fulfill his mission now?"

                    DANNY
Act Three.

                    VIRGIL
The shortest. Ideally building in momentum.
A New Direction puts the protagonist on a
direct collision course with the antagonist.
And it explodes in a Climax —

                    DANNY
High Noon!

                    VIRGIL
As they shoot it out in their final
confrontation. Its consequence is the real
Resolution of the story. The protagonist
succeeds, achieving his mission. Or perhaps
fails. He is left, whatever the outcome,
with profound change.

Danny appears a little overwhelmed.

                    DANNY
Wow. If I could write a movie like that,
Bebe'd be mine.

                    VIRGIL
Any questions?

                    DANNY
Could you explain it again, and make it a
little less abstract?

                    VIRGIL
Sure. Got a double feature we can watch.

Virgil snaps his fingers.

Flames light up a NetherCinema Multiplex logo across the
road map. It separates. Opening like parting curtains.

A wide, shimmering motion picture theater screen is
revealed.

                    DANNY
How'd you do that?

                    VIRGIL
        (shrugging)
I just write the movies, Danny. I leave it
to others to figure out how to shoot them.

                    DANNY
What's showing?

                    VIRGIL
"Gladiator" and "Tootsie."

                    DANNY
Like to see those two duke it out.

                    VIRGIL
One an epic action adventure set thousands of
years in the past, the other a classic
romantic comedy. Both multi-award-winning
audience pleasers. Employing virtually the
same three-act structure coinciding with
development of character.

                    DANNY
Yeah . . . Right . . . A macho Spaniard
enslaved as a Roman Gladiator with an
Australian accent. And a Jewish soap opera
actor convincing everyone he's a she, in
spite of his five o'clock shadow. Exactly the
same.

Virgil lets his sarcasm slide.

                    VIRGIL
Just watch the movies, Danny. And learn.

He begins popping corn over one of the fires as

THE MOVIE SCREEN

Shows credits for "GLADIATOR," Dreamworks SKG,
screenplay by David Franzoni, John Logan, and William
Nicholson.

                    VIRGIL
             (off screen)
We'll cover subplots later, when we talk
about plotting. Just focus on the fifteen
primary points for now.

Russell Crowe as General MAXIMUS walks among legions of
Roman Soldiers, preparing to battle Germanic Barbarians.

VIRGIL AND DANNY

Chow down on popcorn.

                    VIRGIL
Set up. Maximus is the much-loved general of
the Roman army. Nearing the end of the
campaign to conquer the known world, they are
                 (MORE)

VIRGIL (cont'd)
preparing to battle the Germanic Barbarians.
The theme of the movie is stated in a line of
functional dialogue —

DANNY
What kind?

VIRGIL
Functional. We'll discuss purposes of
dialogue later, too.

Virgil flips a kernel and catches it in his mouth.

VIRGIL
An officer says to Maximus, eyeing the poorly
equipped barbarians, "A people should know
when they're conquered." To which Maximus
responds, "Would you know? Would I?" The
theme of the movie, right?

DANNY
The human spirit never gives up.

VIRGIL
There is foreshadowing. Maximus meditates
before going into battle. Visualizing his
wife and child, his hand passes through
golden fields of wheat.

THE MOVIE SCREEN

Shows Maximus leading his men, the bloody battle raging.

VIRGIL
(off screen)
Hell is unleashed.

VIRGIL AND DANNY

Slurp volcanic cokes.

VIRGIL
Commodus arrives conveniently late, feigning
disappointment over having missed the big
fight. He tells his sister Lucilla about his
ambitions to inherit the throne from their
father. Then trains in mock-combat with
exhausted men, another bit of foreshadowing.
It all leads to the Inciting Incident.

DANNY
All that was just Set Up!?

                    VIRGIL
Unfolding as concisely as possible. So the
Inciting Incident, thrusting the story
forward, happens as soon as possible. No
more than twenty minutes into the movie, at
the very latest.

ON THE MOVIE SCREEN

Maximus meets with CEASAR in his tent.

                    VIRGIL
               (off screen)
Telling Maximus he is ailing, that he does
not trust his son Commodus, Ceasar offers him
the throne of the Roman Empire should he die.

VIRGIL

Grins knowingly.

                    VIRGIL
And that one quiet event kicks the action
adventure into high gear. Decision: Maximus
responds that he does not want Rome. He
wants to go home to his beloved wife and
child. Reactions: Not knowing Maximus's
decision, Commodus kills his pop and frames
Maximus for the murder. He declares himself
ruler of Rome, ordering Maximus executed.
But Max gets the jump on his executioners.
Seriously wounded, with what's left of his
strength, he flees home.

                    DANNY
Man! Maximus schwarzeneggered the hell outta
'em, didn't he!?

                    VIRGIL
So we have an obvious good guy and bad.
What's our hero's mission?

                    DANNY
To kick Commodus's butt. Flush him down the
toilet, like his name.

                    VIRGIL
Is that what Maximus declared? Is that what
he's most actively doing, the real need
                    (MORE)

                    VIRGIL (cont'd)
that's driving him? Don't confuse
objectives, which we'll also talk about per
plotting, with mission.

Danny considers a moment.

                    DANNY
               (brightening)
     It's to return to his wife and son.

                    VIRGIL
Exactly. Returning home, he is hit by the
unexpected. They've been murdered. Maximus
collapses. The audience, knowing that his
mission is to be reunited with this loved
ones, wonders, "How will he achieve it now?"

                    DANNY
End of Act One/Reversal.

                    VIRGIL
Maximus finds himself enslaved by a
gladiatorial sports promoter in the
boondocks.

THE MOVIE SCREEN

Shows Maximus sparring with fellow slaves in Africa.

                    VIRGIL
               (off screen)
New Direction. Determined to get to Rome
where Commodus reactivated the games, Maximus
begins training as a Gladiator. So he can
pursue his objective: Avenge the death of his
family.

In the Roman Coliseum, defeating a huge opponent,
Maximus is wildly cheered.

                    VIRGIL
               (off screen)
Decision. Maximus fights bigger foes in the
arena. Becoming an action hero in the eyes
of the Roman people, he reveals his true
identity to Commodus.

DANNY PUMPS HIS FIST

And cheers as well, to Virgil's amusement.

                    DANNY
Dude! Bring on the WWF!!!

                    VIRGIL
Antagonist Reaction. Threatened by Maximus's
celebrity, Commodus keeps him caged and
chained. Which takes us to the Midpoint.

                    DANNY
False resolution. An acceptance or
resignation of fate.

                    VIRGIL
Lucilla goes to Maximus, asking him to lead a
revolt against Commodus.

THE MOVIE SCREEN

Shows weary Maximus in chains. LUCILLA eyes him with
love and admiration.

                    VIRGIL
          (off screen)
He declines, saying he's no longer a leader
of men. He's a slave now, he tells her. He
will die a slave.

DANNY WIPES A TEAR

From his eye.

                    DANNY
Poor Maxie. Resignation.

                    VIRGIL
Decisions and antagonist reactions. Nasty
Commodus pits mad Max against even tougher
opponents. With each victory, his star
shines brighter. Commodus begins killing off
all his political enemies. Assured that a
healthy army of loyal followers are stationed
outside Rome, that his escape has been
carefully arranged, Maximus decides to lead
the revolt.

                    DANNY
The opposite of his statement at the
midpoint.

                    VIRGIL
A decision that'll lead to another event he
doesn't see coming.

THE MOVIE SCREEN

Shows Maximus leaving the walled city. Shocked to see
his officer lynched, he is surrounded by Commodus's
henchmen.

                    VIRGIL
              (off screen)
          Maximus is recaptured. Declared an enemy of
          the state.

                    DANNY
              (off screen)
          And the audience wonders, "How will he
          achieve his mission now?" End of Act Two/
          Reversal.

VIRGIL TURNS TO DANNY

Pleased that he's catching on.

                    VIRGIL
          Act Three. New Direction. Bound, our hero
          is hurled into a direct collision course with
          the villain. Commodus, wanting to be
          worshipped by his people, goes to Maximus,
          telling him he'll fight him in the arena.
          They embrace, mano a mano. Commodus stabs
          him in the kidney.

THE MOVIE SCREEN

Shows them duel in the Coliseum.

                    VIRGIL
              (off screen)
          Maximus accomplishes his objective in the
          Climax.

Weakened, bleeding to death, Maximus slays COMMODUS.

                    AUDIENCE
              (applauding off screen)
          Yea!!!!!!!

VIRGIL AND DANNY

See an AUDIENCE OF GHOULS, GHASTLIES, and CADAVERS,
cheering and clapping, has assembled around them to
watch the movie.

                    VIRGIL
          In the Resolution, has he achieved his
          mission?

THE MOVIE SCREEN

Shows Maximus drop dead. He leaves his body. Hand
passing through golden wheat, he goes to his WIFE AND
CHILD.

IN THE AUDIENCE

Danny turns to Virgil with an expression of unexpected
bliss.

                    DANNY
          Yes, he has. Reunited in the great
          hereafter. The Elysian Fields.

                    GHASTLY
          Oh yeah, like we're really supposed to
          believe there is such a place.

Puff! The cynical ghastly goes up in flames. Disappears
in smoke.

                    VIRGIL
          And in death there's unquestionably profound
          change. Ready for laughs?

THE MOVIE SCREEN

Shows credits for "Tootsie," Columbia Pictures,
screenplay by Larry Gelbart and Murray Schisgal.

                    CADAVER
               (off screen)
          I love that movie!

IN THE AUDIENCE

A euphoric MALE CADAVER dressed in women's clothing
flashes a rotten-toothed grin.

                    VIRGIL
          Danny, take the helm. Saving sub-plots for a
          later discussion, focus on the fifteen points.
          Set Up.

THE MOVIE SCREEN

Shows Dustin Hoffman as MICHAEL teaching a class . . .
Dressed as a tomato, confronting a commercial director
. . . Surrounded by friends, including SANDY AND JEFF, at
his birthday party.

                    DANNY
               (off screen)
          Michael is a teacher, waiter, and unemployed
          actor. Always stressing the importance of
                    (MORE)

                    DANNY (cont'd)
work to friends and students. Yet he keeps
blowing auditions because he's wrong for the
part or hard to get along with. At the
party, there's talk about the impossibility
of raising money to stage Jeff's uncommercial
play.

                    GHOUL
          (off screen)
Shhhhh!

IN THE AUDIENCE

An ANNOYED GHOUL wags a skeletal finger at Danny and
Virgil.

                    GHOUL
You going to yakety-yak through the whole
movie!?

                    VIRGIL
Sorry.
          (whispering)
Any theme suggested in dialogue?

                    DANNY
          (whispering back)
"Instead of being the best actor or waiter,"
Jeff tells him, "be the best Michael."

                    VIRGIL
Success can come from being true to yourself.
Foreshadowing?

                    DANNY
Michael's impulsive behavior. Especially
with women he's sexually attracted to.

                    VIRGIL
What next?

                    DANNY
Michael goes with his friend Sandy to her
soap opera audition, to lend support. But
instead, pissed to learn he's not being
considered for a part he wants in a play, he
runs off, leaving her high and dry.

                    VIRGIL
Leading to the Inciting Incident.

                    DANNY
Michael confronts his agent and demands to
know why he wasn't read for the play? He's
told that he's gotten so difficult to work
with, no one wants him in their shows
anymore. His career might be over.

                    VIRGIL
But the tale it motivates has just been
jumpstarted. Decision?

THE MOVIE SCREEN

Shows Michael emerging as Dorothy on a New York
sidewalk.

                    DANNY
               (off screen)
Disguised as a woman named Dorothy, he goes
to the soap opera audition and, putting a
spin on a part, wins the role his friend
Sandy wanted.

                    VIRGIL
               (off screen)
Mission? A need driving the story?

                    DANNY
               (off screen)
To get work? No. Wait. He's got the job.
So it's to keep working.

IN THE AUDIENCE

Danny cracks up laughing.

                    DANNY
And dog's gotta dress like a hen to do it.
Total drag.

                    GHOUL
Shush!

Virgil and Danny again whisper.

                    VIRGIL
Who's the protagonist?

                    DANNY
Michael, of course.

                    VIRGIL
Is it? Hold on to that thought a moment.
Reactions?

THE MOVIE SCREEN

Shows Michael half-undressed, about to try on some of
Sandy's clothes when she walks in on him.

                    DANNY
                (off screen)
    Michael manipulates Sandy, for his own selfish
    gains.

Michael covers by coming on to her.

                    VIRGIL
                (off screen)
    What about later, with Dorothy?

Dorothy is on the soap opera set, working on a scene.

                    DANNY
                (off screen)
    Dorothy's rehearsing when something
    unexpected catches her by surprise. Julie
    arrives on the set.

Actress JULIE enters, playing the nurse slut. She
smiles and Dorothy looks into her beautiful eyes.

                    DANNY
                (off screen)
    The Michael within reacts, falling madly
    . . . in lust.

                    VIRGIL
                (off screen)
    The audience, knowing the mission's to keep
    working, wonders —

                    AUDIENCE
                (in unison off screen)
    How will it be achieved now!?

THE HOSTILE AUDIENCE

Throws rancid body parts at Virgil and Danny.

                    AUDIENCE
    End of Act One/Reversal!

                    DANNY
    So is Julie the antagonist?

The male Cadaver dressed in women's clothing leans
forward, rolling his cracked eyes, heavy with moldy
mascara.

                    CADAVER
That dear girl? Never! Track the Dorothy/
Michael interrelationship, hun. Isn't
Dorothy the proactive half? Every time she
takes a step forward, isn't Michael doing
something impulsive that screws it up?

                    DANNY
Ah! Dorothy is the protagonist. And
Michael, the antagonist! Talk about good,
bad, and ugly. Whoa.

                    CADAVER
Well done, you got it. Now shut up!

They whisper.

                    VIRGIL
New Direction.

THE MOVIE SCREEN

Shows RON, the soap's womanizing director, degrading
Dorothy and coming on to Julie.

                    DANNY
               (off screen)
Belittled, brushed off, and toyed with,
Dorothy gets a heavy dose of double standards
from men in power.

                    VIRGIL
               (off screen)
Decision?

Standing up for herself, Dorothy gives Ron a severe
scolding.

                    DANNY
               (off screen)
She becomes more assertive . . .

Dorothy talks intimately with Julie in her dressing
room.

                    DANNY
               (off screen)
Advises Julie on her relationships, becoming
her confidant.

                    VIRGIL
               (off screen)
Why?

                    DANNY
                (off screen)
          So she can get closer to her.

                    VIRGIL
                (off screen)
          Sounds like a ploy from the Michael within.
          Antagonist Reaction.

Michael walks away from Sandy, leaving her in tears.

                    DANNY
                (off screen)
          Yeah. Mr. Sensitive goes and does a big
          180, crushing Sandy. Using the same crass
          rap he heard Ron put on Julie.

                    VIRGIL
                (off screen)
          Meanwhile Dorothy . . .

Dorothy improvises on the show. Bewildering the lead
actor, pleasing the female producer.

                    DANNY
                (off screen)
          Champions female empowerment on the show.
          Becoming the shining star of daytime
          television.

                    VIRGIL
                (off screen)
          Which leads to the Midpoint.

Michael enthusiastically talks to his AGENT, who's
looking at him like he's nuts.

                    DANNY
                (off screen)
          Michael goes to his agent and tells him he's
          ready for prime time as Dorothy. She's
          totally his ticket. Wants to be her for the
          rest of his life.

                    VIRGIL
                (off screen)
          False resolution. Acceptance.

                    DANNY
                (off screen)
          Then, new obstacles. Decisions and
          Reactions.

Michael approaches Julie at a party.

                    DANNY
               (off screen)
          Meeting Julie at a party, Michael uses a
          pickup line she told Dorothy in confidence.

Julie throws wine in his face.

                    DANNY
               (off screen)
          And succeeds in getting a face full of fruit
          of the vine.

Dorothy comforts Julie, verging on tears in her
apartment.

                    DANNY
               (off screen)
          Julie tells Dorothy she's followed her smart
          advice, and dumped Ron.

Dorothy tries to kiss Julie. Leaving Julie more
distraught.

                    DANNY
               (off screen)
          Michael within impulsively moves in for a hot
          juicy wet one. Confused and conflicted, Julie
          tells Dorothy she can't see her anymore.

Back at his own place, Michael talks to his bemused
roommate.

                    DANNY
               (off screen)
          Divulging his life's become a screwy mess,
          Michael tells Jeff he wants to stop being
          Dorothy.

IN THE AUDIENCE

Virgil and Danny share a king-sized box of molten
milkballs.

                    VIRGIL
          The opposite of what was expressed at the
          Midpoint. Leading to yet another unexpected
          event that sends the protagonist into a
          tailspin.

                    DANNY
          His agent informs him the network is
          exercising its option on his contract. He
                    (MORE)

                    DANNY (cont'd)
has no choice but to be Dorothy for years to
come. End of Act Two/Reversal, Michael
swears he's going to kill her.

                    VIRGIL
And knowing the mission is to keep working,
the audience wonders —

                    GHOUL
          (annoyed)
When're you going to shut up and watch the
movie!?

                    VIRGIL
Something like that.
          (whispering)
Act Three.

THE MOVIE SCREEN

Shows the people working on the soap opera huddled
together.

                    DANNY
          (whispering off screen)
New Direction. The cast and crew are
informed that a technical snafu is forcing
the show to go live. So Michael seizes the
opportunity for the protagonist versus
antagonist showdown.

In character, the show being broadcast, Dorothy stands
on a staircase and begins improvising a speech.

                    DANNY
          (off screen)
Climax. Dorothy, ranting, whips off her wig
and drops her drawers. Revealing herself to
be Michael.

·Julie goes up to Michael. Slaps him.

IN THE AUDIENCE

The Ghouls, Ghastlies, and Cadavers roar with laughter,
enjoying the movie as much as Virgil and Danny.

                    VIRGIL
Is the mission fulfilled?

                    DANNY
Oh yeah. Because of the brilliance he's
demonstrated playing Dorothy, Michael is
never out of work as an actor again.

THE MOVIE SCREEN

Shows Michael going to Julie when she exits the studio.
He reasons with her, as the familiar voice of a cross-
dressing Cadaver pipes in.

                    CADAVER
          (off screen)
Let's not forget profound change, hun. By
getting in touch with his feminine side, he's
become a better man.

Michael and Julie happily walk away together into the
sunset, down another busy sidewalk.

                    DANNY
          (off screen)
He accomplished his objective, too. Scoring
with a hot actress!

THE AUDIENCE

Of Ghouls, Ghastlies and Cadavers wildly applauds.

                    DANNY
That'll be me and Bebe someday.

                    VIRGIL
No doubt.

Caught in the moment, Virgil's sarcasm goes right
through him as the underworldly audience begins to
disperse.

                    GHASTLY
Hell of a double feature.

                    VIRGIL
Two movies. Creatively showing two very
different journeys. Passing through
essentially the same points of three-act
structure. Beginning, middle, and end.

MAXIMUS AND DOROTHY

Suddenly appear out of nowhere. Arm in arm.

                    MAXIMUS
        Just don't be a slave to it, Daniel. Treat
        it as your guide to finding your own way home.

                    DOROTHY
        Maxie couldn't be righter. Dress it up any
        way your imagination sees fit.

DANNY

Walks away.

                    DANNY
        Yeah . . . Thanks, guys. Absolutely.

                    VIRGIL
            (calling after him)
        Where you going?

                    DANNY
        I'm out of here, dude. You said I could
        leave, anytime I wanted.

He takes off running.

                    VIRGIL
        Wait!

                    DANNY
        I've got to tell Bebe! I'm going to write
        her a great screenplay!

                    VIRGIL
        There's so much more to learn! We barely
        even touched on character!

Danny rushes into a swirling, smoky mist. And
disappears.

Concern crosses Virgil's brow.

EXT. SIDEWALK OUTSIDE ALLEY — NIGHT

Danny sprints out of the shadowy alley.

Face flushed with optimistic excitement, he hurries past
the broken, crackling, red TIMBER'S P ACE neon.

EXT. PENTHOUSE HALLWAY — NIGHT

Dashing out of the elevator, skidding to Bebe's door,
Danny breathlessly knocks on it. No answer. Pounds on
it.

The door partially opens. Bebe peeks out. Surprised.

                    DANNY
    Bebe, baby!

Gleefully wrapping his arms around her before she can
speak, he whisks her back inside.

INT. BEBE'S PENTHOUSE LIVING ROOM — NIGHT

Lights low, seductive jazz again playing.

                    DANNY
    I'm going to bust if I don't tell you!

She gently pushes him away. He ogles the clinging,
revealing lingerie she's almost wearing.

                    DANNY
    Whoa. Talk about bust.

                    BEBE
    Chill a minute. Please . . .

He notices there is an open screenplay on her coffee
table. Two glasses and a nearly empty bottle of
champagne.

She sneaks a guarded glance over his shoulder. Her
bedroom door closes behind him.

He doesn't have to look. Disheartened reality sinks in.

                    DANNY
        (deflated)
    Call me foolish. Call me harebrained. Just
    don't call me late for dinner, right?

She half-smiles. Touches him apologetically.

                    BEBE
    Maybe you should get a cell phone.

He tries to laugh. But can't.

EXT. SIDEWALK OUTSIDE ALLEY — NIGHT

Danny mopes past the red, crackling, TIMBER'S P ACE
neon.

Virgil leans against a brick wall. At the alley's
entrance.

                    VIRGIL
              (kindly)
        What's shakin', sport?

Danny shrugs. Already melancholy.

                    DANNY
        Think I just reached the end of my first act.

Danny enters the alleyway. Barely masking his mirth,
Virgil follows.

INT. ALLEYWAY — NIGHT

They walk through the shadows. Heading back to the
glimmer.

                    DANNY
        Can't say you didn't tell me so, Virgil. I
        got a lot to learn about character.

They vanish in the swirling illumination.

EXT. UPTOWN NETHERWORLD — NIGHT

Starless sky, a deep purple. Molten rocks tower like
uptown high-rises with fiery windows, flanking jagged
stone streets, lava trickling incandescently into
gutters.

They step out of the mist. Danny's dark mood in contrast
to the muffled sound of upbeat Electro-Pyre music.

                    DANNY
              (brooding)
        What is this place?

                    VIRGIL
        Brimstone's, bro. Where the not-so-dearly
        departed come to see and be seen.

Youthful, attractive CARCASSES, trendily dressed to
impress in decayed and frayed rigor mortis chic, are
swarming around the velvet-roped, cavernous entrance to
the nightclub.

                    DANNY
        Don't tell me. My second act reversal's
        picking up stiffs on date-night of the living
        dead.

                    VIRGIL
        Lighten up, already. She's reading someone
        else's script. So what?

                    DANNY
Isn't the reading that bothers me.

                    VIRGIL
Tell you something, Danny-boy, about
protagonists. It's right there in the root
word of the noun. They're proactive. They
take action. One thing they don't do is wimp
out if there's a little competition.

                    DANNY
Right. Damn right! If she's worth having,
she's worth fighting for!
        (thinking it over)
But, if I'm the protagonist of this story,
who's the antagonist?

Not getting an answer, Danny sees Virgil already
approaching the velvet rope. Joining him, he is taken
back by the sight of the red-scaled, cloven-hoofed,
pointy-eared BOUNCER.

                    BOUNCER
Reservations?

                    DANNY
I'm having them.

                    VIRGIL
        (elbowing Danny)
V. Goldman Town and guest.

The bouncer checks the list.

                    BOUNCER
Nope.

                    VIRGIL
        (putting on airs)
Really? I'm absolutely certain my assistant
made them. Perhaps under the name Virgil?

He shakes the bouncer's hand, discreetly handing him a
couple twenties. The bouncers smirks, pocketing the
money.

                    BOUNCER
Sorry, Virg. Going to have to do better than
that. People are dying to get in here.

                    VIRGIL
I'd like to speak to the owner.

>   BOUNCER
>   (smug)
>   You already are.

Not to be dissuaded, Virgil motions for the bouncer to
bend. Whispers in his pointed ear. The bouncer's eyes
narrow. He thinly smiles.

>   BOUNCER
>   Two drink minimum.

He unhooks the velvet rope.

INT. BRIMSTONE'S ENTRANCE — NIGHT

They walk through the cavernous entrance. Electro-Pyre
music pulsates louder. Rocky floor steaming, stalactites
dripping.

>   DANNY
>   What'd you say to him?

>   VIRGIL
>   We should talk about character.

>   DANNY
>   That's what you said to him?

>   VIRGIL
>   In movies, it's most clearly defined by
>   decisive action taken when confronted by
>   obstacle . . .

INT. BRIMSTONE'S — NIGHT

They enter. NuevoNecro motif. Jammed to the rafters.
Danny shouts to be heard over the blasting sound system,
syncopated with throbbing, whirling lights.

>   DANNY
>   You're being evasive!

>   VIRGIL
>   I just want to stay on task. This is one of
>   the most important things I can tell you —

>   HOSTESS
>   Table?

The RAGGEDY HOSTESS, rotten flesh peeling off her high
cheek bones, slinks up to them.

                    VIRGIL
          Dead center.

The hostess escorts them past STYLISH YOUNG CARCASSES on
the make. Chattering. Mingling. Crowding the bar.
Shaking the dance floor. Packing the tables.

She seats them. And slinks away.

                    VIRGIL
          Listen closely . . .

                    DANNY
          So damned loud in here I can barely hear what
          anyone's saying!

                    VIRGIL
          Which makes it the perfect place to discuss
          character.

A skeletal WAITER stops by.

                    VIRGIL
          Bloody Marys.

                    DANNY
          Light on the blood.
               (to Virgil)
          Can't take chances in a place like this.

The waiter clinks away.

                    VIRGIL
          Okay, I'm going to say it again.
               (leaning closer)
          Character in movies is most clearly defined by
          decisive action taken when confronted by
          obstacle. Got it?

                    DANNY
          I'm not sure.

                    VIRGIL
          Check it out.

Virgil points toward

THE BAR

Their words unheard over the music, a GHOULISH HUNK
talks up a PETITE GHOULETTE. She blushes.

                        VIRGIL
                   (off screen)
          Ghoul has an objective. Wants her to go home
          with him, I bet.

                        DANNY
                   (off screen)
          Dude's smooth, and she's kind of timid. Wish
          I could hear the lines he's laying on her.

DANNY

Watches, increasingly intrigued.

                        DANNY
          This's great. Damn! I should've brought
          something to take notes for my screenplay.

A waiter walking by puts a legal pad and pen on the
table. Virgil smiles. Pleased.

                        DANNY
          Cool.

Danny begins jotting down what he's seeing.

AT THE BAR

The ghoulette sweetly shakes her head no.

                        VIRGIL
                   (off screen)
          Hmm. We have an obstacle. Let's see his
          decisive action in response to it.

The ghoulish hunk roughly grabs her. Forces her to kiss
him.

DANNY

Still writing, glances at Virgil in dismay.

                        DANNY
          Smooth? Delete and revise. Insert a
          euphemism for anus.

                        VIRGIL
          The scene's not over. She's got an obstacle
          to deal with now, too.

AT THE BAR

The ghoulette breaks away from the hunk's clutches and
slaps the daylights out of him. His face shatters,
crumbles.

DANNY

Grins, impressed, feverishly writing.

                    DANNY
          Knows how to handle herself, doesn't she?
          Bebe'd love to play a part like that!

                    VIRGIL
          Actions and reactions . . .

                    DANNY
          Speaking louder than words.

                    VIRGIL
          Revealing character.

Danny pauses in his writing.

                    DANNY
          It would help, though, to hear what they're
          saying. Right?

                    VIRGIL
          Sure. But that's getting more into
          functional dialogue. Let's just stay focused
          on character for now. A few minutes ago, my
          objective was to get us past the ropes.

                    DANNY
          And big red was the obstacle.

                    VIRGIL
          So I decided to take action. What did it
          reveal about my character?

                    DANNY
          You're persistent. Aggressive. You think on
          your feet. Don't take no for an answer.

The waiter returns with their drinks.

                    DANNY
          What did you whisper to him, anyway?

                    VIRGIL
          Let's talk fundamentals.

                    DANNY
          That's what you said to him?

                    VIRGIL
          Protagonist and antagonist.

                    DANNY
          You're being evasive again.

                    VIRGIL
          Listen up. This is important. Your
          protagonist, through the course of your
          story, should exhibit a wide range of
          recognizable human traits —

                    DANNY
          Well, duh. Antagonists should too.

                    VIRGIL
          Oh? Really?

Virgil's eyes narrow. Mischievously.

The Electro-Pyre music transforms into a classic
thriller refrain by John Williams. Low. Ominous.
Steadily building. De dum . . . de dum de dum . . .
Like a dorsal fin slicing through water.

Oblivious, Danny sips his drink.

                    DANNY
          Mmmm. Spicy.

A great white SHARK smashes up through the rocky floor,
razor-tooth jaws wide open. Danny shrieks . . .

                    DANNY
          Ahhhhhhhh!!!!!!!!!

Drops his drink. Horrified carcasses run like hell.

Virgil bonks the shark on the nose. It retreats back
through the floor.

Danny's pale. Holding his chest.

                    VIRGIL
          Great antagonist? Yes. Wide range of human
          traits? I don't think so.

Danny glances down at himself. And frowns.

INT. MEN'S REST ROOM — NIGHT

Wearing Spider-man boxer shorts, Danny rinses his pants
in a crater sink. His legal pad and pen on the counter.

                    VIRGIL
          See, the audience needs to be able to relate
          to the protagonist . . .

                    DANNY
Identify with him.

                    VIRGIL
On a human level. With the way he evolves.
His growth. His arc.

                    DANNY
How do you mean?

                    VIRGIL
In film, dramatic stories are often about
change, the impact something has on someone.
A character enters a story with one attitude,
and ends it with another. At the beginning
of "The Godfather," for example, young
Michael wants no part of the family business.
He's rebelling.

                    DANNY
But by the end, he's running it. Not just
part of the establishment. He is the
establishment.

                    VIRGIL
It's that rite of passage . . . not the
violence, betrayals, and tests of allegiance
. . . the audience relates to. How as
children, through no design of our own, we
oft-times fall into the footsteps of our
parents.

Danny wrings his pants out. Shakes them.

                    DANNY
Yeah. Here's this dude who begins lying,
cheating, killing. He even orders a hit on
his own brother. Yet I feel for him.

                    VIRGIL
Empathy. Even in an animated movie with a
lion cub protagonist or a talking train,
you've got to establish it. You want that
bond. To get it you need to reveal, within
the arc, as full a range of human traits and
characteristics as possible.

                    DANNY
What if you don't?

                    VIRGIL
Something terrible happens. The audience
rapidly loses interest in the story. Simply
doesn't care.

                    DANNY
But what about antagonists, then?

Danny puts his dripping pants under a wall-mounted
gargoyle blow dryer.

                    DANNY
That shark in "Jaws." We understood him,
didn't we? He was motivated by his primal
instincts, to eat and survive.

                    VIRGIL
No question about it. Yet there's a world of
difference between grasping something, and
relating to it. While you got why the shark
did what he did . . .

                    DANNY
It was those three guys on the boat I
empathized with.

                    VIRGIL
Exactly. Your point is well taken, though,
audiences should understand the antagonist.
And the best human ones are as
multidimensional as the hero. It's just that
the audience doesn't necessarily need to be
able to identify with him.
        (emphasizing)
Or it.

                    DANNY
An antagonist can be an it?

                    VIRGIL
Can be all sorts of things. Think about
interrelationships in some of the movies
you've enjoyed.

Danny glances out a window. Sees through it the
netherscape of fiery high-rises.

                    DANNY
How about "Die Hard"?

                    VIRGIL
Good choice. Great action. Clear-cut good
and bad guys. Who was the protagonist?

                    DANNY
Easy. John McClane. The cop Bruce Willis
played.

                    VIRGIL
What was his mission?

                    DANNY
To stomp the terrorist thieves that took over
the skyscraper.

                    VIRGIL
That was an objective. Remember, a mission
involves a personal need that motivates a
protagonist while pursuing objectives.
McClane said it . . . we're touching on
functional dialogue here . . . right in the
set up of the movie.

                    DANNY
Ah. To reconcile with his wife.

                    VIRGIL
The antagonist generating obstacles getting
in his way was . . . ?

                    DANNY
Hans Gruber. Bad to the bone.

                    VIRGIL
Urbane, articulate, worldly. The perfect
oppositional force to clash with a streetwise
cop.

                    DANNY
As the old saying goes, "the hero's only as
good as the villain."

                    VIRGIL
And don't you ever forget it! Did McClane
achieve his mission?

                    DANNY
Hell yeah!

Danny clenches his fist triumphantly.

                    DANNY
Snuffed Gruber and his Euro-thugs. Then
drove off to live happily ever after with his
bride.

                    VIRGIL
Until the sequel, anyway. Let's do another
one. "Saving Private Ryan." Protagonist?

                    DANNY
Tom Hanks' Captain Miller.

                         VIRGIL
          Mission?

                         DANNY
          To find Ryan and protect him.

He pauses. Catching himself.

                         DANNY
          Wait. That was an objective. His mission
          involved his wife, too. He repeated it
          throughout. It was to return home to a
          peaceful life with her.

                         VIRGIL
          What generated the obstacles? What was the
          oppositional force?

                         DANNY
          War. The ultimate antagonist to a man
          wanting a tranquil life.

                         VIRGIL
          Did Miller achieve his mission?

                         DANNY
          No. The war killed him.

He pauses in solemn reflection.

                         VIRGIL
          "A Beautiful Mind." Protagonist?

                         DANNY
          John Nash. Russell Crowe again.

                         VIRGIL
          His mission?

                         DANNY
          He said it often. It was to create an
          original thought.

                         VIRGIL
          Antagonist?

A shabby DRUNK CARCASS enters the rest room. Gazing at
them, he rolls his cracked, bloodshot eyes, and mumbles
to himself.

                         DRUNK CARCASS
          Sharks . . . Spiderman boxer shorts . . .
          Life in hell . . .

The carcass staggers into a stall.

                         DANNY
          I'm pretty sure the antagonist was
          schizophrenia.

                         VIRGIL
          For a man desiring clarity of mind, hard to
          imagine an oppositional force that could be
          greater, isn't it?

His pants dry, Danny puts them back on.

                         VIRGIL
          Did Nash achieve his mission?

                         DANNY
          He learned to manage his mental illness,
          created the game theory of economics, and won
          a Nobel Prize.

Danny smiles. Almost with a sense of pride.

                         DANNY
          So yeah. Big time.

He grabs the legal pad and exits the rest room with
Virgil as a deep groan comes from within a stall.

                         DRUNK CARCASS
                    (off screen)
          I like the nightlife . . . I like to
          boogie . . .

EXT. DOWNTOWN NETHERWORLD — NIGHT

They mosey through another part of town, under the
starless, deep purple sky. The hour's grown late. The
jagged, stone streets are quiet. Only a smattering of
fires burn in molten rock office building windows.

                         VIRGIL
          You never fought in a war, battled
          schizophrenia, or shot it out on a high rise.
          Yet even now, thinking back about those three
          protagonists elicits an emotional response.

                         DANNY
          Guess I related to them, on a human level.
                    (glancing at his pad)
          What I need to know now, is how to create
          them?

                    VIRGIL
          The key to that highway, Danny-boy, is
          research and imagination. If you want to
          make your characters credible and
          multidimensional, you have got to meet them
          and get to know them. Inside and out.
          Research, man. It's what fuels the
          imagination.

                    DANNY
          Okay. Where do I begin?

They pause at broken stone steps, leading up to the
columned entrance to the Netherworld Public Library.

                    VIRGIL
          Might start at the library.

INT. N.P.L. — NIGHT

Swirling dust floats through the air.

They stroll among towering stacks of ragged books,
tottering as far as the eye can see, flanking endless rows
of cobwebbed reading tables.

                    VIRGIL
          Whether protagonist or antagonist, explore
          books about characters like the one you want
          to write about . . .

INT. PERIODICAL ROOM — NIGHT

Virgil hands a yellowed, faded magazine to Danny. It
flakes apart in his hands.

                    VIRGIL
          Read journals, magazines, newspaper
          articles . . .

INT. COMPUTER ROOM — NIGHT

Dilapidated cubicles, cobwebbed computers.

                    VIRGIL
          Look at photos. Surf the net . . .

INT. LIBRARY OFFICE — NIGHT

Hollow-eyed behind shattered glasses, her straw-gray
hair in a tight bun, the decomposed remains of a
LIBRARIAN lifelessly sit at a desk.

                         VIRGIL
          Interview people that do what your characters
          do.

                         DANNY
               (to the librarian)
          What's it like to work around so many
          publications? Is it exciting? Stimulating?
               (getting no answer)
          Miss?

He nudges her. Her head falls off. Hitting the desk
with a thump.

                         DANNY
          Apparently not.

INT. AUDIO-VISUAL ROOM — NIGHT

Rows of unraveled, corroded tapes and films fill the
shelves.

                         VIRGIL
          Watch films with similar characters in
          comparable situations.

                         DANNY
          In other words, do your homework.

Virgil smiles. Nods.

INT. COMMUNITY ROOM — NIGHT

Virgil's at a cobwebbed lectern. Danny, writing in his
legal pad, sits front and center in the decrepit
auditorium.

                         VIRGIL
          Along with all the research, begin compiling
          a list. A laundry list, I like to call it.
          Of biographical tidbits to color the
          character.

He clicks on a laser-pointer.

                         VIRGIL
          Put some of these on it. Make up more of your
          own.

Directs attention to

A DISPLAY

Showing a long list of items to consider.

1. Character's Name:
2. Nickname:
3. Gender:
4. Age:
5. Physical Appearance:
6. Occupation:
7. Marital/Romantic Status:
8. Sexual orientation:
9. Friend(s):
10. Place of birth:
11. Places lived:
12. Parents:
13. Siblings:
14. Education:
15. Religion:
16. Ethnicity:
17. Socio-Economic Status:
18. Politics:
19. Tastes in Music:
20. Tastes is Movies, Theater, TV:
21. Tastes in Clothes:
22. Favorite Foods and Drink:
23. Hobbies:
24. Talents & Skills:
25. Personality Traits:
26. Psychological Traits:

Mission:

What is his/her greatest need?
What motivates him/her to achieve it?
What key action/activity defines it?

Obstacle:

What is his/her greatest weakness/fear?
What central problem is created by it?
What key action/activity defines it?

VIRGIL

Clicks off the laser-pointer.

                    VIRGIL
        Questions? You, in the back of the room.

Danny turns. He sees a DEAD GUY with a bloody pencil
stuck in his forehead has his hand up.

                    DEAD GUY
Should a list like that ever really appear on
the pages of a script?

                    VIRGIL
That's off the subject, but no. You only
want to write what the audience can see and
hear. That list is too long to read on the
screen. I took liberties for educational
purposes.

                    DEAD GUY
What about all that dribble — I mean, bio.
Should all of it ever really appear in a
story?

                    VIRGIL
Probably not. But you might find an
unexpected place where you can use it. What
it will do is force you to get to know your
characters, and help spark your imagination
when you need it. Here's one of the ways it
can work: Contrasting.

Dead guy pulls the pencil out if his forehead. Takes
notes.

                    VIRGIL
Don't ever have the leads . . . even if
they're best buds . . . with the same traits
or points of view. Boring! Last thing you
want between them is harmony. Opposites
attract, right? Well in movies, it attracts
drama.
          (pausing, ruminating)
Say you're William Goldman, writing "Butch
Cassidy and the Sundance Kid." You decide
Butch knows how to swim. So to contrast it,
the Kid doesn't. Remember that classic scene
on the cliff?

                    DANNY
What about that weakness/fear thing under
obstacle?

                    VIRGIL
Create something that magnifies the
protagonist's opposition. Some sort of
problem he must overcome to confront the
antagonist. In "Jaws," Chief Brody was
afraid of the ocean. In "Die Hard," John
McClane —

49.

                    DANNY
        Had a fear of flying. Of heights.

                    VIRGIL
        Made things harder on them, didn't it? See,
        in movies, when it comes to obstacles, the
        more the merrier. Adds to the excitement
        and . . .

                    DANNY
        Defines character.

                    VIRGIL
        You bet. Know what else can help define the
        protagonist, Danny? And antagonist, for that
        matter?

A shout comes from the back of the auditorium.

                    DEAD GUY
        Supporting characters!

Dead guy smiles smugly. And crams the bloody pencil back
in his forehead.

EXT. DOWNTOWN NETHERWORLD — PREDAWN

They stroll away from the library, the glimmer of a fiery
orb peeking above the molten horizon. Danny's legal pad
in hand.

                    VIRGIL
        Dead guy's right. Just be careful your
        supporting characters aren't a bunch of
        excess baggage, cluttering everything up. If
        they're in your story, they should serve a
        specific purpose.

                    DANNY
        Like in "Die Hard." How Al, the cop with the
        radio, cheers McClane on. Man, he is super-
        supportive!

                    VIRGIL
        Goes beyond being a pep squad. Their most
        important functions are often narrative.

                    DANNY
        Want to lay some examples on me?

                    VIRGIL
        Obi-Wan Kenobi in "Star Wars."

                    DANNY
May the force be with you!

                    VIRGIL
He teaches Luke Skywalker the ways of the
Jedi. And by showing him Princess Leia's
dilemma, gets him to take action.

                    DANNY
So by mentoring and motivating, Obi-Wan moves
the story forward.

                    VIRGIL
In "Shindler's List," Itzhak, Oscar's
accountant, answers his questions about
traditions among Eastern European Jews, and
the realities of life and death in the camps.

                    DANNY
Which in turn, answers questions in the minds
of the audience.

                    VIRGIL
Chris, in "Platoon," finds himself in the
crossfire of feuding Sergeants Elias and
Barnes . . .

                    DANNY
Who personify Oliver Stone's theme of good
and evil as it might exist on the battlefield.
The war raging within.

                    VIRGIL
And countless romantic interests in thousands
of flicks. Who function as supporting
characters to give the protagonist a reason
to live. To believe. To pursue his mission.

Danny pauses at the entrance to a cavernous alleyway.
The fiery orb inches higher on the distant horizon.

                    VIRGIL
That's the thing about missions in movies.
Whether it's a desire to go home or to find
self-worth. The most meaningful ones in the
most memorable films are about an aspect of
love.

Danny thoughtfully makes a note in his legal pad.

                    VIRGIL
Separates us from the other animals in the
kingdom, my friend. Lies in the heart of all
                    (MORE)

               VIRGIL (cont'd)
drama. The need to be loved. By others, as
well as ourselves.

Danny nods. And looks up from his pad at the fiery orb.

               VIRGIL
What're you thinking, sport?

Danny stares. As if challenging the orb to burn his
eyes.

               VIRGIL
Danny? What're you doing? Danny?
     (getting no response)
Danny . . . ?

The orb flares. Brightly blinding.

INT. BEBE'S PENTHOUSE LIVING ROOM — NIGHT

The bright glare of an end table lamp.

               BEBE
Danny?

Half asleep on Bebe's sofa, Danny partially opens his
eyes. Squints.

               BEBE
Danny . . . ?

Screenplay in hand, Bebe gently shakes him.

               BEBE
     (sweetly)
Sleepy-head. Rise and shine.

               DANNY
     (groggy)
Guess I nodded . . . Had this totally
whacked-out dream.

               BEBE
I read your script.

He sits up. Now fully awake.

               DANNY
Yeah? Tell me . . .

               BEBE
Well, the structure's sound.

                              DANNY
          Maybe a little pat?

                              BEBE
          Got some good characters beginning to happen.

                              DANNY
          Bebe. Baby. If you really want to help me,
          be honest with me. That's the way we've
          always been with each other, right? So lay
          it on me, cut to the chase.

                              BEBE
          It really sucked.

Danny's taken back. Then chortles, amused.

                              DANNY
          Good one. Got me. But all kidding aside —

                              BEBE
          All kidding is aside. Blew the big one.

                              DANNY
                    (crestfallen)
          Didn't have to be that honest with me.

                              BEBE
          I mean, come on. You've found your
          structure, but so what? The scenes within it
          endlessly poke, plod, and meander. This is
          supposed to be a motion picture, Danny. Not
          a slide show. Gotta give a reason to turn
          the page. Put a little oomph in it!

                              DANNY
          Is that a screenwriting term?

She gives him a look.

                              BEBE
          Frankly, Danny, I can see why you dozed. I
          was kind of struggling to stay awake through
          it, myself.

                              DANNY
          There's a fine line, Bebe. Between honesty
          and brutality.

                              BEBE
          And the dialogue coming out of characters'
          mouths . . . Gawd! How am I supposed to play
          such dribble?

                    DANNY
I guess what you're telling me, is the
screenplay needs a little work.

                    BEBE
Is that what this is supposed to be? It
doesn't look like a screenplay. Doesn't read
like one. I know a screenwriting term you
ought to use. Format.

Danny hangs his head. The phone rings. Bebe snaps it
up.

                    BEBE
          (into phone)
Yeah . . . ? Just did.
          (turning away, lowering voice)
Not even close. I'll get back to you, okay?

Hangs up. Turns back to Danny with a forced smile.

                    BEBE
My manager. Total Type-A.

She takes Danny's face in her hands. Sweet as can be.

                    BEBE
Ooo, kiss kiss. Don't take it so hard.
There's some really original writing here.

                    DANNY
Think so?

                    BEBE
Know so!

He brightens.

                    BEBE
Like some of the words. It's very clever the
way you spelled them.

He smiles weakly.

INT. TIMBER'S PLACE — NIGHT

A gravelly Tom Waits love song again on the jukebox.
Danny is back, perched on a wobbly stool. He wearily
flips through his screenplay, open on the bar.

                    BARTENDER
The usual?

                    DANNY
        Seems that way, doesn't it?

The bartender pours him a shot of tequila. Lends him an
ear.

                    BARTENDER
        Problems with the writing?

                    DANNY
        I don't know. Maybe I should just throw the
        towel in the ring. I'm no screenwriter.
        Been fooling myself.

Danny shakes his head regretfully. Glances at the
scattered Down and Outers conspiring over pitchers of
beer.

                    DANNY
        Who was it that said, "Tell me not in
        mournful numbers, Life is but an empty
        dream?"

                    VIRGIL
        Longfellow.

Danny startles. Sees Virgil, as if out of nowhere,
sitting beside him.

                    VIRGIL
        "For the soul is dead that slumbers, And
        things are not what they seem." A Psalm of
        Life.

Danny's speechless.

                    VIRGIL
        Somebody reach their midpoint?

                    DANNY
            (to the bartender)
        Where'd he . . . ?

But returning the bottle to the mirrored shelf, the
bartender has his back toward him.

Danny glares at Virgil.

                    DANNY
        Midpoint!?

                    VIRGIL
        False resolution.

                    DANNY
     I don't understand.

                    VIRGIL
     The protagonist feels he's found what he's
     looking for, and accepts it. Or fears he'll
     never find it, and is resigned to —

                    DANNY
     I know what a midpoint is, dammit! What I
     don't understand is —

                    VIRGIL
     Interesting, isn't it? The way the midpoint
     reflects the inciting incident.

                    DANNY
     What inciting incident?

                    VIRGIL
     Meeting me, Danny-boy. That was the inciting
     incident in this —

                    DANNY
     My life is not a screenplay!

                    VIRGIL
     Good! Conflict. That's what they like to
     hear.

                    DANNY
     Who the hell are you!?

                    VIRGIL
     Just a supporting character, bro. Trying to
     help you.

                    DANNY
     Help yourself!

Danny slams a couple bills on the bar and storms out,
leaving behind the script. Virgil grabs it, chasing
after him.

                    VIRGIL
     But it's not over. New decisions have to be
     acted on!

EXT. SIDEWALK OUTSIDE ALLEY — NIGHT

Hurrying past the broken TIMBER'S P ACE neon, Virgil
catches up with Danny next to the entrance of a shadowy
alleyway.

                    VIRGIL
Not bad. We had some drama going in there,
didn't we?

                    DANNY
Call it what you want. But I am not happy.
I'm confused. And I do not want to see you.

                    VIRGIL
Oh, now we're back to trite talk. Does the
phrase "on-the-nose" mean anything to you?

                    DANNY
What? We're going to discuss dialogue now or
something?

                    VIRGIL
Loose quips sink scripts.

Danny glowers. Virgil grins, offers him back his
screenplay.

                    VIRGIL
It's one of my possible functions, as a
supporting character. Rousing you back toward
your mission.

Danny hesitates. Then takes it, unable to deny his
feelings.

                    DANNY
Why can't she be like other girls? Want
something simple like diamonds or flowers?

                    VIRGIL
Never, ever make things easy on the
protagonist. Right, pal?

                    DANNY
She's just so damn beautiful.

Screenplay in hand, he turns to enter the dark alley.

                    VIRGIL
Not the best choice, cinematically.
Repetition burns the audience out, so you
want to keep showing them fresh stuff.

                    DANNY
Then what?

Virgil motions toward the curb.

A NETHERCRAFT SPORTS COUP

Inferno-dynamic, made of chromium alloy, it hovers in
midair by a ticking parking meter.

>   VIRGIL
>   Let's book. I'm out of change and the
>   meter's about to expire.

Seamless doors with tinted windows wing open.

>   DANNY
>   Where you taking me this time, Hades City
>   Hall?

>   VIRGIL
>   Don't want to give it away . . .

He steps off the curb, crossing to the driver's side.

>   VIRGIL
>   Wouldn't be good screenwriting.

INT. NETHERCRAFT — NIGHT

Virgil is behind the wheel, putting the coup into gear.

>   VIRGIL
>   Hope you went potty. Got a long dive ahead
>   of us.

Danny smirks, buckling into the passenger seat, his
script on his lap.

>   DANNY
>   Thing like this could happen, only in the
>   movies.

>   VIRGIL
>   You catch on fast.

He flips a switch.

EXT. SIDEWALK OUTSIDE ALLEY — NIGHT

The coup rises, arcs downward. A mega-drill extends
from its front grill.

Blast off. Plowing into the street, it plunges right
through like a hard rock miner.

58.

INT. NETHERCRAFT — NIGHT

The ride's shaky. Layers of earth accelerate past the
coup's rattling windows.

                    VIRGIL
          Both an art and a craft, Danny.

He glances at Virgil, carefree behind the wheel.

                    DANNY
          This coup?

                    VIRGIL
          No, man. Functional dialogue.

                    DANNY
          I write it the way I hear it. The way people
          talk.

                    VIRGIL
          Big freakin' mistake.

That gets Danny's attention.

                    VIRGIL
          Hemming and hawing. Beating around the bush.
          Digressing on and on and on, without anything
          particular to say. For most, all that
          rambling's just another mundane way to pass
          the time of day. It's a good thing they're
          not paying for it.

                    DANNY
          Talk is cheap?

                    VIRGIL
          Movie tickets aren't.

Danny thinks about that one.

                    VIRGIL
          Give the audience their money's worth. For
          real-speak, they can go to the laundromat.

                    DANNY
          Then what should I write?

                    VIRGIL
          Told you already, bro. It's called
          functional dialogue. Don't write the way
          people yammer, interpret it instead. Create
          an illusion of it. That's the art. The
                    (MORE)

VIRGIL (cont'd)
craft . . . like you never heard this one
before . . . is that it serves specific
purposes in your movie.

DANNY
So all the people in the story can
communicate.

VIRGIL
Yeah, but not with each other. To the
audience. Dialogue, when it's working, can
help advance the plot, foreshadow coming
events. Assist in clarifying missions,
objectives, themes, growth, and change. It
can provide needed exposition, when it can't
be cinematically shown.

DANNY
Sounds like a supporting character.

VIRGIL
In a way. Strong dialogue can help reveal
emotion, relationship, and personality.
Bolster tone, sustain mood. Through verbal
imagery, it can evoke sight and sound. And
as if that's not enough, on top of all those
functions it might do, is the one that it has
to do. Entertain.

DANNY
Not asking too much, is it?

VIRGIL
No one said it was going to be easy.

EXT. INNER EARTH ATMOSPHERE — DAY

Plunging through the last layer, they enter the inner
earth's atmosphere. The mega-drill withdraws.

The coup soars downward in wide, circular patterns.
Through yellowish gases, rippling with fumes of scarlet,
emerald, and lavender, reflecting the flaring midday orb.

INT. NETHERCRAFT — DAY

The ride smoothens. Virgil flicks another console
switch.

VIRGIL
Check it out. In-descent movies.

A fuzzy pool of light is projected between them.

Adjusting a knob brings two attractive HOLOGRAMS, ROCK and DORIS, into focus.

Rock approaches Doris. Kisses her on the cheek.

> HOLOGRAM ROCK
> Hi, Doris.

> HOLOGRAM DORIS
> Hi, Rock.

> HOLOGRAM ROCK
> You look good.

> HOLOGRAM DORIS
> Thanks. Thanks. Been working out.

> HOLOGRAM ROCK
> Cool. It shows. Um, are we uh, on for . . .
> you know . . . Friday night?

> HOLOGRAM DORIS
> Uh, yeah. Sure.

Restless, Danny looks

OUT THE WINDOW

At the inner-earth atmosphere. Something distant, sluggishly wallowing through the gaseous expanse, appears out of place.

A glob-like mass. Turning in their direction.

> HOLOGRAM DORIS
> (off screen)
> I mean, if you're still into it?

THE TWO HOLOGRAMS

Ramble on.

> HOLOGRAM ROCK
> 8:00?

> HOLOGRAM DORIS
> If that's good for you, yeah, okay.

Danny groans.

Virgil pushes a button. The holograms freeze.

                    DANNY
        So lifelike.

                    VIRGIL
        Too lifelike. Realistic, but just barely
        functional. And not even close to being
        entertaining. Watch them play it out again.

                    DANNY
        Do we have to?

Virgil pushes the button.

Rock approaches Doris. Kisses her on the cheek.

                    HOLOGRAM ROCK
        If I told you, Doris, you had a great body,
        would you hold it against me?

Danny snickers, already amused.

                    HOLOGRAM DORIS
        Careful now, Rock. I'm naked under these
        clothes.

                    HOLOGRAM ROCK
        Oh, I'll be careful, all right.

                    HOLOGRAM DORIS
        Screw that.

                    HOLOGRAM ROCK
        Friday at eight?

                    HOLOGRAM DORIS
        I'm holding you to it.

Danny cracks up laughing.

Virgil freezes the action.

                    VIRGIL
        Same scene, but more like a movie. Skipping
        salutations and getting to the point.
        Revealing personality, relationship, tone,
        and objectives.

                    DANNY
        Got to try that line on Bebe.

Danny writes a quick note on his script.

Virgil pushes the button.

Waving a cowboy hat, Rock is decked out in denim, riding
a bucking bronco. He's thrown. Hits the ground hard.

He painfully picks himself up. Limps over to Doris,
sitting on a fence.

                    HOLOGRAM DORIS
          Mustang gave you quite a ride there, cowboy.

                    HOLOGRAM ROCK
          Held on. Best I could.

Virgil freezes the action.

                    VIRGIL
          That, partner, is what you call show and
          tell.

                    DANNY
          Big no-no?

                    VIRGIL
          Might be what is said in real life. But in a
          movie, totally bites. You want to avoid
          dialogue that repeats what was just seen,
          that tells the audience what is going on.
          Because it adds nothing new to the story.

Virgil pushes the button.

Waving a cowboy hat, Rock is decked out in denim, riding
a bucking bronco. He's thrown. Hits the ground hard.

He painfully picks himself up. Limps over to Doris,
sitting on a fence.

                    HOLOGRAM DORIS
          Not getting any younger, cowboy.

                    HOLOGRAM ROCK
          Didn't stop my old man. Damned if it'll stop
          me.

Virgil freezes the action.

                    VIRGIL
          A few simple lines of dialogue that addressed
          obstacle and clarified mission. Without
          mentioning either the ride or the horse.

                    DANNY
          Because the audience just saw it.

Virgil pushes the button.

The holograms are sipping cups of coffee.

>   HOLOGRAM ROCK
>   I can see how happy he makes you.

>   HOLOGRAM DORIS
>   Yeah, he really does. It's a great feeling.

Virgil freezes the action.

>   VIRGIL
>   On-the-nose. Characters saying, in an
>   obvious manner, what they feel.

>   DANNY
>   No good?

>   VIRGIL
>   Right. Totally uncinematic.

Virgil pushes the button.

The holograms are sipping cups of coffee.

>   HOLOGRAM ROCK
>   Look at you. Got a glow-on or what?

>   HOLOGRAM DORIS
>   It's like, when I'm with him, I can't stop
>   smiling. I sing when I should talk. Laugh
>   when nobody's joking. I want to race up
>   stairs, three steps at a time. Shout with
>   glee to the world from my rooftop!

>   HOLOGRAM ROCK
>   Wow. I gotta get me a Puppy.

Virgil freezes the action.

Danny is grinning.

>   DANNY
>   Corny, but conveyed happiness.

>   VIRGIL
>   And was experiential.

>   DANNY
>   Defined as . . . ?

64.

                    VIRGIL
     Dialogue reflecting something the character
     experienced. Creating pictures, outside of
     the scene, in the minds of the audience.

                    DANNY
     Through concise verbal imagery.

                    VIRGIL
     Speaking of which . . .

Virgil pushes the button.

Midday heat. Rock, shirtless, polishes his customized
Harley Davidson Motorcycle while tank-topped Doris
watches.

                 HOLOGRAM ROCK
     Got an increased camshaft, for lift and
     duration. Good for the long haul. Hugs even
     the most dangerous curves.

                 HOLOGRAM DORIS
     Must be exhilarating . . .

She takes the cloth from him. Rubs finish on the engine.

                 HOLOGRAM DORIS
     Having that much power between your legs.

They make eye contact.

                 HOLOGRAM ROCK
     Want to climb on? Find out?

Virgil freezes the action. Danny's on the edge of his
seat.

                    DANNY
     For some reason, Virgil, I don't think it's
     that motorcycle they're talking about.

                    VIRGIL
     Subtext, my friend. What's implied beneath
     the line. Mix it up with innuendo, gets kind
     of interesting, doesn't it?

                    DANNY
          (musing)
     Me and Bebe. Wind blowing through our
     hair . . .

                    VIRGIL
     Okay. Let's say you've avoided all the
     pitfalls. Dialogue's flowing like fine wine.
     Gotta ask yourself one last question. One
     that's so big, it's a potential deal breaker.

                    DANNY
     Does Bebe like Harleys?

He makes another note on his script.

                    VIRGIL
     No, bro. Is it dramatic? Is your dialogue
     dramatic?

Virgil pushes the button.

The illusion of a posh restaurant appears.

The two holograms are seated at a table. Menus in hand.

                    HOLOGRAM DORIS
     What do you have a taste for, Rock?

                    HOLOGRAM ROCK
     Four bedrooms, three baths. On an acre of
     prime woodland. Away from the crime, grime,
     and congestion of the city.

                    HOLOGRAM DORIS
     Sounds like where I grew up. All that's
     missing is a collie.

She diverts her eyes to the menu.

                    HOLOGRAM DORIS
     It'd be so great for the kids, wish we could
     afford it.

                    HOLOGRAM ROCK
     Be careful what you wish for.

She glances up. A hologram WAITER crosses to their
table, showing Rock a bottle of champagne. He nods.

                    HOLOGRAM DORIS
     What are you telling me?

                    HOLOGRAM ROCK
     Just thinking out loud. About the sort of
     place I'd love to come home to. After a long
     day slaving away in my corner office.

                    HOLOGRAM DORIS
          You got the promotion!?

The bottle pops open. The waiter pours. They raise
their glasses in a toast.

                    HOLOGRAM ROCK
          To the life we now share. And all that
          tomorrow will bring.

Virgil freezes the action. And smirks, sarcastically.

                    VIRGIL
          Pretty exciting, wasn't it? Dude?

Danny is again looking

OUT THE WINDOW

At the inner-earth atmosphere. The glob-like mass is
moving toward them. And it's gaining in size and
momentum.

                    VIRGIL
               (off screen)
          Earth to Daniel.

VIRGIL

Nudges him.

                    DANNY
          Huh? Oh, sorry.
               (indicating out the window)
          There's this —

                    VIRGIL
          Whatever. I can easily understand why you
          lost interest. But at least try to stay on
          task with me, will you?

Danny shrugs.

                    DANNY
          Dialogue sorta sounded functional.

                    VIRGIL
          But it lacked that one key element mandatory
          in all drama. Conflict.

                    DANNY
          Can't have characters screaming at each other
          all the time.

VIRGIL
Course not. But a scene that goes on too long, with characters seeing eye to eye, is the surest route to audience boredom.

DANNY
How do you handle the alternative?

VIRGIL
Keep the point/counterpoint going. Have them disagreeing. Get them arguing, debating, and challenging. Doesn't mean they have to always be shouting, or in each other's faces. They just have to be like Butch and Sundance, haggling jumping from the side of that cliff.

Virgil pushes the button yet again.

VIRGIL
Let's revisit America's fun couple. With a few revisions.

The two holograms are seated at a table. Menus in hand.

HOLOGRAM DORIS
What do you have a taste for, hun?

HOLOGRAM ROCK
Four bedrooms, three baths. On an acre of prime woodland. Away from the crime, grime, and congestion of the city.

HOLOGRAM DORIS
Sounds like where I grew up. All that's missing is a collie.

She diverts her eyes to the menu.

HOLOGRAM DORIS
Like we could afford it.

HOLOGRAM ROCK
Maybe we can.

She glances up. A hologram WAITER crosses to their table, showing Rock bottle of champagne. He nods.

HOLOGRAM DORIS
What are you telling me?

Annoyed, she promptly waves the waiter and champagne away.

                    HOLOGRAM ROCK
Just thinking out loud. About the sort of
place I'd love to come home to. After a long
day slaving away in my corner office.

                    HOLOGRAM DORIS
You took the promotion?

                    HOLOGRAM ROCK
Thought you'd be pleased.

                    HOLOGRAM DORIS
With what? You putting in fourteen-hour
days, instead of the usual twelve? And now,
you want to add a commute?

                    HOLOGRAM ROCK
Gimme a break. Said yourself, how great it'd
be for —

                    HOLOGRAM DORIS
What would be great . . . !
     (catching herself, lowering voice)
Is for the kids to see their dad at home
every once in a while.

                    HOLOGRAM ROCK
Who the hell do you think I'm doing this for?

                    HOLOGRAM DORIS
How should I know? Certainly not me. I
don't know what you're doing in that office
all day.

                    HOLOGRAM ROCK
Providing for you and the children!

                    HOLOGRAM DORIS
Provide them with a father!

Virgil freezes the action.

                    VIRGIL
Point marries counterpoint . . .

                    DANNY
And their union is conflict.

                    VIRGIL
     (to the Holograms)
Thanks, guys. Outstanding work.

Danny and Virgil applaud their performances.

Podiums appear. The holograms reanimate. Clutching Oscars.

                    HOLOGRAM DORIS
        You like me! You really like me!

Rock elbows in front of her.

                    HOLOGRAM ROCK
        I want to take this opportunity to express my
        sincere gratitude to the academy for . . .
        Wait . . .

He sees Virgil promptly reaching for the console switch.

                    HOLOGRAM ROCK
        Don't cut me off here! This is my moment! I
        want to thank my agent, the wonderful crew in
        wardrobe, my high school drama te —

Virgil flicks the switch. The two holograms dissolve
into oblivion.

                    VIRGIL
        One other thing. Avoid monologues. They're
        a convention of theater and fiction, not film.
        Unless it's a courtroom drama, for example,
        where it's organic to deliver a stirring
        summation, lengthy speeches tend to slow down
        the drama by grinding the progression of
        moving pictures to a halt. If you find
        yourself writing one —

                    DANNY
        Break it up with another character
        interjecting something.

Danny smiles smugly.

                    VIRGIL
        Or with action, or some sort of related
        imagery. Which brings us to the all-
        important subject of . . .

Danny looks back

OUT THE WINDOW

The mass is suddenly upon them.

                    VIRGIL
              (off screen)
        Plotting.

A gargantuan WINGED SLUG. Drooling, its hideous mouth
gapes open, slurping up the craft like a noodle.

DANNY

Freaks.

                    DANNY
          Virg!

He sees

THROUGH THE WINDOW

A giant slimy tongue, broken and filthy teeth clamping
down.

DANNY AND VIRGIL

Hold on their seats. They plunge into a violent spin.

Darkness.

EXT. INNER EARTH ATMOSPHERE — DAY

The slovenly slug swallows.

A satisfied grins spreads across its humongous lips.

                    SLUG
          Mmmm.

It wallows on toward the flaring orb.

Letting out a baritone belch.

INT. NETHERCRAFT

The rumbling belch resonates in the darkness.

                    DANNY'S VOICE
          Lemme guess. You're going to use this
          opportunity to tell me the function of
          plotting.

                    VIRGIL'S VOICE
          Matter o' fact . . .

A light beam lands on Danny's perturbed face. Cast from
the miner's hardhat Virgil is now wearing.

                    VIRGIL
          Like everything in your story, plot for
          maximum impact on the audience. Drama's
                    (MORE)

                    VIRGIL (cont'd)
    manipulative, man. You got to scheme to keep
    viewers involved. Because the function of
    plotting is to make sure, from scene to
    scene, that they're always wanting to know
    what's going to happen next?

He hands Danny a hardhat.

                    VIRGIL
    Simple enough?

INT. SLUG'S STOMACH

The doors of the marooned coup wing open.

Danny, screenplay in hand, and Virgil climb out, wearing
protective jumpsuits and boots. Beams from their hard
hats light the vastness of the slug's slime-dripping
innards.

Membranes throb. Digestive fluids puddle and bubble.

                    DANNY
    Another fine mess you've gotten me into.

                    VIRGIL
    What can I tell you? Setting's part of
    plotting. You want to come up with places,
    locations, that'll visually enhance the
    drama.

He looks around.

                    VIRGIL
    Near as I can see, there's only two ways
    outta this one.

                    DANNY
    But —

A sudden gurgle distracts them. A whirlpool sucks waste
with a rumble, squeal, and puff of gas.

                    VIRGIL
    No buts about it. We take the high road.

They begin their trek through sticky stomach acids.

Littered with chewed remnants of body parts and a few
garbage bins, road signs, and political campaign
posters.

                    DANNY
So, plot. Sounds to me a lot like structure.

                    VIRGIL
Goes hand in hand. Structure arranges
scenes. Plotting goes on within them.

                    DANNY
What constitutes a scene?

                    VIRGIL
Beats showing a sequence of events, often
with a beginning, middle, and end all their
own.

                    DANNY
And a beat is . . . ?

                    VIRGIL
A moment. Or a unit of action. To be
dramatic, someone in the scene needs to have
an objective they act upon. And it should be
met with —

                    DANNY
Obstacle. Conflict.

                    VIRGIL
Always the essence, isn't it?

Behind them, unseen and unheard by them, a horribly
mangled

INGESTED FREAK

Struggles out of the slime. Bloody tissues and organs
droop from gaping holes in its gnawed flesh. It sniffs.
Leers.

                    FREAK
Screenplay . . .

Fixating through dead eyes, it begins to stalk

DANNY AND VIRGIL

Sludging through abdominal goo. Oblivious to the danger
behind them, Danny holds his screenplay close to his
chest, safeguarding it from being soiled.

                    DANNY
Keeping an audience wanting to know what'll
happen next . . . What's the trick to that?
                  (MORE)

                    DANNY (cont'd)
Delaying showing if the objective in the
scene is met?

                    VIRGIL
That's one way. Before you even get there,
take care not to start the scene too early.
Like your overall story, begin it where it
needs to. With the thrust of event already
in motion. Focus on what's important to
reveal to the audience. Otherwise, right off
the bat, their minds will begin to wander.

                    DANNY
And once that happens, you probably lose them
forever.

As the freak trudges closer

TWO MORE OF THE INGESTED

Squirm up from the slush. Deadly. Half-eaten.

DANNY AND VIRGIL

Slosh on.

                    VIRGIL
Create any number of cliffhangers. End
scenes with questions that are unanswered.
Issues unresolved. Give the viewers the
expectation of pending consequence and
reaction.

                    DANNY
Like at the end of that scene in "Tootsie"?
Where Dorothy impulsively leans over to kiss
Julie?

                    VIRGIL
Awesome cliffhanger! The audience wants to
know what will happen next because Julie's
left so conflicted. If she decides to get hot
and heavy later on, it could change the whole
direction of the movie.

                    DANNY
Not to mention the rating.

                    VIRGIL
In thrillers and action-adventures, you can
create ticking clocks. In those genres the
more harrowing the better.

                    DANNY
        Like in "Silence of the Lambs." How Clarice
        must act within a certain time frame to
        rescue the Senator's kidnapped daughter.

                    VIRGIL
        The audience grows anxious to see what will
        happen next, watching her butt heads with
        Hannibal Lecter.

The vile stalkers are joined by SIX MORE. Murderous
desire in their mauled eyes.

                    VIRGIL
        Another strong device is to reveal something
        a character we care about doesn't see.

                    DANNY
        Sort of like sharing a secret with the
        audience.

                    VIRGIL
        Yeah. One that glues them to the edge of
        their seats. Gets them waiting with bated
        breaths, eager to find out what it's leading
        to?

The gang slogs nearer. ANOTHER THREE merge into their
ranks. Clicking. Snapping. Wheezing.

                    DANNY
            (spooked)
        Hear that?

Virgil glances at dripping membranes, pulsating around
them.

                    VIRGIL
        Sluggo's probably got a touch of indigestion.

A psychotic giggle.

                    FREAKS
        Screenplay . . .

They turn.

The disgusting dozen are within striking distance.
Twitching to kill. Glints of weaponry in their mangled
hands.

                         DANNY
                    (masking fear)
          Feel like I wandered into a Michael Jackson
          video.

                         VIRGIL
          Going to have to do better than that, pal.
          Movies have to show audiences what they can't
          see on TV.

They back away. Not taking their eyes off the freaks
keeping pace with them step by step.

Drooling. Snarling. The freaks are poised to rip them
apart, limb from limb.

                         VIRGIL
          The dramatic arts have always been about
          pushing the envelope, taking things to the
          edge . . .

                         DANNY
          I'm feeling edgy.

                         VIRGIL
          Look how far Sophocles took "Oedipus Rex."
          Wrote it over fifteen hundred years ago, and
          folks still flock to see it. Alan Ball, a
          little more recently, did he flinch and blink
          when he wrote "American Beauty"? Not even
          close. Audiences came, awards followed.

                         DANNY
          What's that got to do with these freaks
          wanting to turn us into Chop Suey?

                         VIRGIL
          Each new generation of dramatists, and
          screenwriters are no different, faces the
          same ultimate challenge.

                         DANNY
          Survival?

                         VIRGIL
          Audiences, Danny, have seen it all. To
          really get them wanting to know what will
          happen next, you've got to surprise them with
          the shock of the new. The unexpected.
          You've got to dare to take things farther
          than those that came before, and be bold
          enough to confront the limit.

                    DANNY
What're you saying? A proper protagonist
would stand up to these mongrels and fight?

                    VIRGIL
Only if he's stupid.

Danny shoots him a look out of the corner of his eye.

                    VIRGIL
Run like hell.

They flee. Plowing through the slush. The gruesome dozen
in manic pursuit.

                    FREAKS
Screenplay . . . ! Screenplay . . . !

                    VIRGIL
Careful with it!

Pressing with Virgil against the rancid current, Danny
holds his script high. Away from splashing viscous
debris.

                    VIRGIL
Note the way this is unfolding!

Danny slips, falls.

A blade-wielding freak lunges for him.

Virgil dashes. Jerks Danny up out of harm's way. Back
on his feet, they skidaddle.

                    DANNY
What . . . !?

The freak goes under. Drowns in gross gunk as his
comrades trample over him.

                    DANNY
How they're trying to kill us!?

                    VIRGIL
How the writer's detailing the descriptive
action! Ends this scene with a pivotal beat!

They slosh forward with all their might, like convicts
from a chain gang battling a swamp.

                    DANNY
Sure as hell has me anxious to know what
happens next!

                    VIRGIL
          Up ahead! The esophagus!

The slug's belly narrows to a curved, wet wall with a
portal.

The deranged posse gains ground. Snarling. Cackling.
They claw at Danny's back. Reaching out . . .

                    FREAKS
          Screenplay!

                    VIRGIL
          Squeeze!

Virgil shoves Danny through the portal.

Danny out of view, Virgil presses his back to it.
Shields it. Lowers his voice.

                    VIRGIL
          Chill, dammit!

The freaks slide to a sloshing halt. Cower in his
presence.

                    VIRGIL
          Not yet. There's more to do.

With a stern look of warning, Virgil squirms into the
portal.

INT. ESOPHAGUS

Squeezing in behind Danny, Virgil instantly affects
frantic.

                    VIRGIL
          Climb! They're right behind us!

They scamper up through the slippery, wet tunnel.

Script in hand, Danny glances over his shoulder.

                    VIRGIL
          Don't look back! Hustle!

EXT. INNER EARTH ATMOSPHERE — DAY

The slovenly Winged Slug, sauntering through the
atmosphere, gets a lump in its throat.

                         VIRGIL
                      (off screen)
             Watch the back of the tongue!

Suddenly bug-eyed, the slug chokes, gags, retches.

                         DANNY
                      (off screen)
             I'm stuck!

An even more HUMONGOUS SLUG flaps over.

Applies an efficient Heimlich maneuver with its wings.

DANNY AND VIRGIL

Are ejected like projectiles from slovenly's mouth.

                     DANNY & VIRGIL
                      (plummeting)
             Ahhhhhhhhh!!!!!!!!!

THE TWO GIGANTIC WINGED SLUGS

Flutter off together through the gaseous sky.
Silhouettes in the flaring orb.

                       HUMONGOUS
             Told you a million times, sluggy. Chew your
             screenwriters, before you swallow 'em.

                         SLUG
             Sorry, daddy.

EXT. SCARLET FIELDS — DAY

Fields of scarlet grass roll like waves. Incandescent
in the hot breeze.

Danny and Virgil hit the ground with a clump.

Danny gets to his feet.

Looks at his screenplay. Appears undamaged.

                         DANNY
             Bizarre, they'd be after this.

                         VIRGIL
             Just a coincidence, I guess. That all those
             desperate inkslingers would be running amuck
             in Sluggo's belly.

Danny helps Virgil up. Scrutinizing.

                    DANNY
I thought coincidence in plotting was a weak
device.

                    VIRGIL
Plenty of terrific stories are jumpstarted by
coincidences. "American Beauty." Lester's
dissatisfied with his life. He meets Rick,
purely by chance. And watching Rick give his
boss the big brush-off, decides to follow his
example and take control of his own destiny.

                    DANNY
Yeah, but inciting incidents aside, events
should always be instigated by the
protagonist, antagonist, or one of their
supporting characters.

Virgil straightens his clothes.

                    VIRGIL
We still need to discuss subplots.

                    DANNY
Are you being evasive again?

                    VIRGIL
No way.

Virgil glances away from him, at something in the
distance.

                    VIRGIL
You want to avoid repetition in your
plotting, too. Reveal something new to your
audience in every scene.

                    DANNY
Gimme a break. I ask a direct question, you
can at least give me a direct answer.

                    VIRGIL
If you're going to create one or more
subplots . . . and not all movies have to have
them . . . be sure they support the principal
story and its themes. Instead of taking away
from them.

                    DANNY
Like supporting characters function with a
lead.

                    VIRGIL
Supporting characters are typically who the
subplots are about. Like mini-stories within
the bigger one. Containing beginnings,
middles, and ends all their own.

They step on to a yellow path. Winding through rolling
hills of scarlet grass, beneath gaseous skies, it leads
to a

WHITE RECTANGULAR MONOLITH

Indistinct. At the apex of the vanishing point not far
away.

VIRGIL

Motions for Danny to follow.

                    VIRGIL
We're off.

                    DANNY
From gizzard to wizard?

                    VIRGIL
"Die Hard."

                    DANNY
          (alarmed)
Say what!?

                    VIRGIL
Jeb Stuart and Steven E. De Sousa's seminal
screenplay . . .

                    DANNY
Oh. Right. For a second I thought you
meant —

                    VIRGIL
. . . Illustrates perfectly how subplots
function. Remember John McClane's mission?

                    DANNY
To reconcile with his wife, Holly.

                    VIRGIL
Theme?

                    DANNY
Love. The lengths that one will go through
in the name of it.

                    VIRGIL
There are five distinct subplots in the movie.
Showing five notions of love. The first
subplot involves Holly's coworker, Ellis. He
rivals John for her affections and betrays
him, an event that gets him killed. The
second tracks Al.

                    DANNY
A cop who loves his job, but misses working
the street. Stuck behind a desk, he feels
impotent. Because he's been unable to draw
his gun since accidentally shooting an
innocent in the line of duty.

                    VIRGIL
Till the end. When he blows crazy Karl away,
saving John's life.

                    DANNY
Regaining his manhood.

                    VIRGIL
Bringing a little cowboy mythology to the
shoot-em-up.

The white monolith looms closer.

                    DANNY
Guess it's pointless to ask what's ahead?

Virgil keeps walking. Danny shrugs alongside him.

                    VIRGIL
Karl is subplot three. After John offs his
brother, he's hell-bent for revenge.

                    DANNY
Irrational over his unnatural love for his
sibling.

                    VIRGIL
Four involves the reporter Richard. He
jeopardizes John and Holly by interviewing
their kid on the news.

                    DANNY
Totally self-absorbed, the creep is in love
with himself.

                    VIRGIL
Blindly ambitious. Doesn't care who he hurts
as long as he gets the scoop.

                    DANNY
Ends up getting walloped, right in the nose.
By Holly on live TV!

                    VIRGIL
Antagonist Gruber gives us subplot five.
Greed. In love with money, he engineers the
heist of the skyscraper. With total
disregard for human life.

                    DANNY
Left splattered all over on the sidewalks.
Plummeted. Compliments of John's love for
Holly.

                    VIRGIL
Five subplots incited, thematically linked,
and resolved.

                    DANNY
Beginning, middle, and end. Cool.
How about ensemble dramas? Aren't they made
up entirely of entwining subplots?

                    VIRGIL
Some are. Like "Magnolia." Strands all
involve characters desperate to connect with
others. Validation of self-worth. Did you
see "Dazed and Confused"?

                    DANNY
Yeah. The kids are struggling to fit in.
With those they regard as peers, for better
or worse.

                    VIRGIL
"American Graffiti"?

                    DANNY
Everyone's on the verge of transition.
Coming to terms with where their lives are
going.

                    VIRGIL
Ensembles. Threads bound by theme.

Danny scratches his head. A little overwhelmed.

                    DANNY
So much to creatively consider when writing a
screenplay. Structure, character. Dialogue
and plotting. Conflict. Descriptive action.

                    VIRGIL
    One other thing. That's mandatory.

Danny glances at him. Inquisitively.

                    VIRGIL
    Don't look at me. Look at this.

He indicates the monolith. It's a towering

BOUND SCREENPLAY

Propped up straight before them.

                    VIRGIL
    You've got to make it read right on the page.

                    DANNY
    Yeah. Bebe had a gripe about that.

                    VIRGIL
    Listen, when you submit a script to a
    producer, development exec, or agent, the
    first person to read it will probably be a
    Story Analyst or Reader. They have a ton of
    reading to do, day in, day out. Remember
    that number I mentioned in the bar?

                    DANNY
    Thirty-five thousand.

                    VIRGIL
    That's your competition. Guarantee you, if
    your script's a headache to read, cluttered
    with useless jargon and amateurish in its
    layout, it's a sure pass, no matter how good
    the story.

                    DANNY
    How do I make it look professional?

                    VIRGIL
    Standard Screenplay Format. Simple to read.
    Easy on the eye. Lots of white space on the
    page. Like this one.

He shifts attention to the monolithic script.

                    VIRGIL
    Notice that the cover is plain card stock.
    No fancy frills or artwork. Pages are
    photocopied on three-hole paper and bound
                    (MORE)

                    VIRGIL (cont'd)
with two one-and-a-quarter inch number five
solid brass fasteners, one on the top and one
on the bottom.

Virgil tries to turn to the first page. Too heavy to
budge.

                    VIRGIL
Come on, help me out here, will you?

Danny sets his own script on the ground. Helps Virgil
open the big one.

                    VIRGIL
Check out the title page. Clean. Title
centered about a third of the way down. "By"
and the author's name centered below it.

                    DANNY
I see the contact info in the lower right
corner, but there's no date or mention of
which draft this is.

                    VIRGIL
Because this is a spec screenplay. Written
speculatively, hopefully to sell. Even if
it's been around for ages, the reader should
think it's the most current draft, hot off
the presses.

They turn to the first page.

                    VIRGIL
Take a look at the text. You want to set the
left margin at one-and-a-half inches and the
right at one inch. Top, one inch to the
body, and half-inch to the number. Leave
anywhere from one-half to one-and-a-half
inches at the bottom, depending on your page
break.

Scratching his head, Danny looks right, then left.
Down, and then up. At seemingly nothing in particular.

                    VIRGIL
I know what you're thinking. The spacing's
way off on the page we're on.

                    DANNY
               (smirking)
We're on? The real question I'm pondering,
Virgil, is what are you on?

                        VIRGIL
It's because Continuum, Danny. The publisher
of this manual . . .

                        DANNY
What manual?

                        VIRGIL
The one the script we're in is part of. They
had to modify the format, so it'd fit more
neatly on the —

                        DANNY
Stop! First you tell me we're in a
screenplay, then some sort of how-to book!
What is gonna come out of your mouth next!?

                        VIRGIL
Fonts.

                        DANNY
Great. Now you're talking dirty . . .

                        VIRGIL
Talking twelve-point ten-pitch courier, as
opposed to the nine-point Continuum's using
here.

Danny steps closer. Looking over the giant page.

                        DANNY
What if I want to use colors, bold face, or
italics to make the script attractive, so
words stand out.

                        VIRGIL
Black courier only, man. Industry standard.
Simple. Clean. Clear.

                        DANNY
Don't see much capitalized, either.

                        VIRGIL
Nope. You want to capitalize the slug
lines . . .

                        DANNY
Slug . . . ? Oh, like that thing that
swallowed us.

                    VIRGIL
Slug lines are scene headings. You also want
to capitalize characters' names when they're
first introduced and above dialogue when they
speak. Like ours are here and when you and
Bebe were introduced on page one.

Danny shoots him a look.

                    DANNY
Page one . . . ? There you go, talking like
my life's a screenplay again.

Virgil puts a patronizing arm around his shoulder.

                    VIRGIL
Maybe it is, Dano. For educational purposes.

He winks. And turns back to the giant page.

                    VIRGIL
For dialogue, set left at three inches and
right at two-and-a-half, more or less. Don't
fret if it's a bit off. Tab the name of the
character speaking about four-and-a-fifth
inches. Always keep them in line, like ours
are here. Never center them.

                    DANNY
Should I use (CONTINUED) and/or (MORE) when a
character's speech is broken up by action?

                    VIRGIL
No. Only use it when a character's speech is
interrupted by a page break. Like what
happened at the bottom of page eighty-three,
and top of eight-four in this script.

                    DANNY
This one? The one you're under the delusion
we're in?

Danny smirks. And Virgil smirks right back at him.

                    DANNY
Okay. What if the software I'm using
automatically breaks the page on a slug line?

                    VIRGIL
Move it yourself to the next page. Never
separate a slug line from the description it
accompanies.

DANNY
What if I want to do a flashback?

VIRGIL
Just set it up with some functional dialogue
or a transitional image.

DANNY
Yeah. I remember, I was working on my
screenplay.

Danny pauses. Thinking back.

INT. BACHELOR PAD — LATE NIGHT

The moon casts amber light through the window. Crossing
the corner of a shadowed poster for a movie featuring a
Hollywood goddess from an era long gone.

Danny is exhausted. Working at his computer.

DANNY
(voice over)
Man, it was late. Really late.

His head slightly bobs. Fighting the sleep impulse.

DANNY
(voice over)
I was beyond tired.

He gives in. Slumps. Putting his head on his desk, his
eyelids drift shut.

A distant telephone is heard ringing.

DANNY
(voice over)
Odd . . .

EXT. SCARLET FIELDS — DAY

Danny snaps out of his reverie.

DANNY
Maybe we really are just a couple of flunkies
in a . . .

The annoying ringing continues. Virgil tries ignoring
it.

                    DANNY
              (shrugging)
         Whatever. Going to illustrate phone
         conversations?

Virgil digs in his pocket for his cell phone.

                    VIRGIL
              (into cell phone)
         Yo?

INT. BEBE'S PENTHOUSE LIVING ROOM — NIGHT

Bebe is comfy on her sofa. Sipping champagne and looking
at a celebrity magazine with a glossy photo of herself on
the cover.

                    BEBE
              (into phone)
         What gives, Virgie? Gotten him to agree?

EXT. SCARLET FIELDS — DAY

Virgil turns his back toward Danny. Puts his hand over
the phone.

Danny can't hear what he's saying.

                    VIRGIL
              (into phone)
         Not yet.

INT. BEBE'S PENTHOUSE LIVING ROOM — NIGHT

Bebe yawns. Feigning indifference.

                    BEBE
              (into phone)
         Oh well. I'm sure something else will come
         along.

EXT. SCARLET FIELDS — DAY

                    VIRGIL
              (into phone)
         Give me a few more minutes.

He clicks off. Pocketing his phone, he turns back to
Danny. Masking.

                    VIRGIL
         Telephone solicitor. Let's move on to
         parentheticals.

                    DANNY
Ah. Those words in parentheses, sometimes
underneath a character's name when he's
speaking.

                    VIRGIL
Put them on the line directly below the
character's name, maybe half an inch to the
left. Use them sparingly to suggest a simple
action or emotion.

                    DANNY
              (emphatically)
Like this!

                    VIRGIL
Exactly. Anything more, write it as
descriptive action.

Danny stifles an incredulous laugh.

                    DANNY
Man! I'm beginning to totally buy into this.
I'm in a screenplay! I don't even exist off
the page! Wait, I don't see CUT TO's between
scenes.

                    VIRGIL
I don't recommend using them. They clutter
up a script. Make it look longer than it
really is. Besides, writing a new slug line
implies the cut. So don't waste the space.

                    DANNY
What about camera angles?

                    VIRGIL
Not your job. Don't even mention the camera
in your script. Let the director and
cinematographer decide where to put them.

                    DANNY
I've seen them in published scripts and on
the internet.

                    VIRGIL
Those are production drafts. When you're
writing a spec, like this one, write only
master scenes that imply overall views of a
setting.

Danny surveys the scenery.

                    VIRGIL
Within them, Danny, you can always use mini-
slugs to direct the mind's eye. Like below
on this page, and into the next.

                    DANNY
So weird, dude. Freaking unusual.

Bemused, he glances down at himself. Virgil quickly
creeps behind the monolith.

                    DANNY
Guess we really are just a couple of guys,
roaming through the realm of the scripted.

Virgil puts his shoulder to

THE TOWERING SCRIPT

And gives it a swift shove. It topples.

                    DANNY
Functioning to edu —

Splat! It lands on Danny. Like a flyswatter whacking a
bug.

VIRGIL

Picks Danny's screenplay up off the ground. Flips it
open.

                    VIRGIL
Chump.

He takes out his cell phone. Dials.

                    VIRGIL
           (into cell phone)
Bebe, baby. Our dreams are about to come
true.

He turns off the cell phone. Looks at the toppled
monolith.

                    VIRGIL
Didn't see it coming, did you sport?
           (grinning smugly)
Must be the end of the second act.

He laughs to himself as

A CREVICE

Unzips in the air near him. With a cocky swagger, Virgil
steps through it and vanishes.

DANNY'S HAND

Inches out from under the gigantic script.

                    DANNY
               (straining)
          And the beginning . . . of the third . . .

Lifting with all his might

DANNY

Squirms out from under the weighty script.

Pissed, he sees

THE CREVICE

Still open.

Danny scrambles to his feet and leaps through it as it
begins to zip closed.

INT. BEBE'S BOUDOIR — NIGHT

Puffy pink pillows adorn the frilly, oversized bed.
Flowery bouquets dress the wallpaper. Glamour photos of
Bebe surround a vanity mirror.

The crevice, still zipping, hangs in midair.

Danny squirms out of it. Gathers his senses as the
crevice zips the rest of the way up and disappears.

                    BEBE
               (off screen)
          Detained?

                    DANNY
               (bewildered)
          Bebe . . . ?

Hearing Bebe and Virgil's voices, he tiptoes to listen
at the partially open door.

                    VIRGIL
               (off screen)
          That's what he told me to tell you. What can
          I say? Kid's kind of weird.

Danny tenses. Anger setting in.

INT. BEBE'S PENTHOUSE LIVING ROOM — NIGHT

Virgil, nonchalant, with his feet crossed on the coffee
table, has Danny's script in hand as Bebe, in evening
clothes, sashays to a cocktail cart.

                    BEBE
            (indicating the script)
     Didn't even copyright it, or get it
     registered.

                    VIRGIL
     Can't imagine what he was thinking.

                    BEBE
     But you know how to get the forms.

                    VIRGIL
     Write, or stop by, the Registration Office.
     Writer's Guild of America, West. 7000 West
     Third St. Los Angeles, CA. 90048. Or
     follow the links at www.wga.org online.

                    BEBE
     Guild registration's only valid for five
     years.

                    VIRGIL
     Can always renew.

                    BEBE
     What about copyright protection?

                    VIRGIL
     Good for life. Plus seventy years.

She smiles. Glances at herself in a headshot on the
mantle as she mixes martinis.

                    BEBE
     Movie stars are forever.

                    VIRGIL
     Nevertheless. Here's the address:
     Application Forms. Copyright Office. Library
     of Congress. Washington, DC. 20599. Or
     download them from lcweb.loc.gov/
     copyright.forms.

                    BEBE
     So easy. Any expense?

                    VIRGIL
      Registration's twenty dollars for non-guild
      members. Copyright costs the same.

                     BEBE
        Seems, though, it's a weak system.

INT. BEBE'S BOUDOIR — NIGHT

Danny's jaw bitterly tightens as he listens at the open
door.

                     BEBE
                (off screen)
        Because it's still no guarantee of protection
        in a court of law.

                    VIRGIL
                (off screen)
        True. If called upon . . .

INT. BEBE'S PENTHOUSE LIVING ROOM — NIGHT

Bebe shakes the mixture with a flourish.

                    VIRGIL
        . . . all the Guild will do is exhibit
        registered materials in its signed, dated,
        and sealed envelope.

                     BEBE
        And even with the copyright, unless scenes or
        pages have been lifted verbatim, a writer's
        got a lengthy, potentially expensive battle
        trying to prove his idea's been stolen.

                    VIRGIL
        I'll drink to that!

INT. BEBE'S BOUDOIR — NIGHT

Danny cringes.

                     BEBE
                (off screen)
        Can't think that's a good thing.

INT. BEBE'S PENTHOUSE LIVING ROOM — NIGHT

Martinis in hand, Danny's screenplay tucked under
Virgil's arm, they stroll through sliding doors. Virgil
smirks.

                    VIRGIL
     Depends which side you're on. How much
     money's behind you.

EXT. VERANDA — NIGHT

A warm breeze stirs plants and outdoor furnishings.
Twenty stories high, open air, with panoramic views of
the nighttime sky, Hollywood Hills, and sparkling lights
of L.A.

                    VIRGIL
     Fearing lawsuits, some companies won't even
     take a submission unless it's from an agent
     or a lawyer.

                    BEBE
     What about managers?

                    VIRGIL
     By law they're not supposed to seek or obtain
     work for clients. Unlike agents and lawyers,
     they don't have to be licensed or pass bar
     exams to practice.

                    BEBE
     Then what do they do?

                    VIRGIL
     Some produce. Others just provide guidance
     and open doors that create the opportunities
     for submissions.

INT. BEBE'S PENTHOUSE LIVING ROOM — NIGHT

Danny creeps through Bebe's Living Room. He pauses near
the open sliding doors.

                    BEBE
          (off screen)
     And competition's fierce.

                    VIRGIL
          (off screen)
     Better believe it. A motivated, connected
     manager can be a valuable ally. Just watch
     out for hacks.

Unseen by them, Danny clenches his fists.

EXT. VERANDA — NIGHT

Virgil has Danny's script in one hand, a martini in the
other.

                    BEBE
     Can't you submit your properties to a company
     or producer, representing yourself?

                    VIRGIL
     Absolutely.

He looks her in the eye. Affects a swagger.

                    VIRGIL
     If they're willing to take it.

                    BEBE
     So what's the best defense?

                    VIRGIL
     A good offense. Before you show anything
     . . . whether it's to a lawyer, agent,
     manager, producer, or company . . . find out
     what you can about them. Make sure that
     they're reputable.

                    BEBE
     Are you?

He winks. Teasing.

                    VIRGIL
     Depends what you're after.

                    BEBE
     Should've guessed.

She smiles back. Playing along.

                    VIRGIL
     Contact the library at the Academy of Motion
     Picture Arts and Sciences at 310—247—3020.
     Ask them to pull folders. Call the Writer's
     Guild at 323—951—4000, ask if an agent or
     company is signatory. Keep a paper
     trail . . .

                    BEBE
     Detailed records.

                    VIRGIL
     Of anyone and everyone reading your material.

He holds up Danny's script.

                    VIRGIL
And only show your work when it's actually
ready. Not just some idea that's still
percolating.

                    BEBE
Danny's got a fantastic concept.

                    VIRGIL
No question. Yet others could have similar
ones going. Like I told him. Ideas are all
around us. There, practically for the
asking.

                    BEBE
But finding a screenplay that works is like
mining for gold.

He gives her an inquisitive look.

                    BEBE
I read the scene in Timber's.

                    VIRGIL
        (laughing)
To our naive little buddy, Danny.

VIRGIL

Raises his martini.

                    VIRGIL
Who's done me a great service by doing none
of the above to protect himself . . .

INT. BEBE'S PENTHOUSE LIVING ROOM — NIGHT

Danny is so angry he's about to explode.

                    BEBE
        (off screen)
What do you mean?

                    VIRGIL
        (off screen)
All I've got to do is give his script a page
one rewrite.

EXT. VERANDA — NIGHT

Virgil steps closer to Bebe.

                    VIRGIL
Put my name on it.

                              BEBE
                         (surprised)
                    Just your name?

                              VIRGIL
                    Register and/or get it copyrighted.   And
                    begin showing it to our network of
                    connections.

Danny vehemently bursts onto the veranda.

                              DANNY
                    When hell freezes over!

Virgil and Bebe reel back.   From Danny and from each
other.

                              VIRGIL
                         (freaked)
                    Look what the wind blew in.

                              DANNY
                    Next time, don't forget to zip up.

Virgil frowns.

                              VIRGIL
                    Story of my life.

                              DANNY
                    Hand over the script, Virgil.

                              VIRGIL
                    Yeah.   Sure . . .

Virgil clutches the screenplay.

                              VIRGIL
                    But first, let's you and me talk.

                              DANNY
                    I've heard enough talk!   Remember what you
                    said, movies are about what people do.

Reaching behind his back . . .

                              DANNY
                    Well guess what Danny-boy's going to do?

He whips out a pistol.   Virgil freaks.   Bebe scowls.

                              BEBE
                    Since when do you carry a gun?

                    DANNY
              (shrugging)
          Plot convenience, I guess.

                    BEBE
          Weak dramatic device, Danny. Got to set it
          up to keep it credible.

                    DANNY
          I'll give you credibility!

Danny aims the weapon at Virgil.

                    VIRGIL
              (cautiously)
          Easy, sport . . . This isn't what it looks
          like. I'll spell it out for you —

                    DANNY
          Can only go by what I see and hear.

                    BEBE
          I'm afraid he's right, Virgie. Good
          screenwriting gives us action. Not
          explanation.

                    VIRGIL
          Who's side are you on!?
              (to Danny)
          If you'll just let me tell you!

                    DANNY
          Show in a movie. Don't tell.

                    VIRGIL
          This isn't one yet! We're still in
          screenplay form!

                    BEBE
          Point he's trying to make, Danny, is you can
          still revise. This story doesn't have to
          turn out this way.

                    DANNY
          Sorry. Script or flick, this is the climax.
          Showdown between the good guy and the bad.
          And at this range I can't miss.

He cocks the pistol.

                    BEBE
          Then it's a weak ending, in need of tension,
          maybe a last minute twist. An audience won't
                    (MORE)

                    BEBE (cont'd)
feel suspense if the protagonist has the
upper hand.

                    VIRGIL
Wait, Bebe. Hold on a second.

Virgil feigns confusion.

                    VIRGIL
You think I'm the antagonist?

                    DANNY
              (sarcastically)
No, I think you're a figment of my
imagination. About to be blown to make-
believe smithereens for trying to swipe an
idea existing only in the convolutions of my
mind.

He inches his finger on the trigger.

                    VIRGIL
              (cowering)
Somehow, I don't quite think that's a capital
offense.

                    DANNY
In the world of my story it is.

                    BEBE
Boys!

She steps between them.

                    BEBE
I might have the solution. You got a terrific
concept. Right, Danny?

                    DANNY
A fantastic one, Bebe. To quote.

                    BEBE
Virgil, you got the ways and means to make it
happen on paper.

                    VIRGIL
I wasn't named V. Goldman Towne for nothing.

                    BEBE
Me, I'm a star. The prized element desired
to get greenlit. To turn a property into an
actual movie.

She postures. As if finding her mark on camera.

                    BEBE
          Unless I've grossly misread the whole
          situation, fellows, the three of us want the
          same thing.

Danny and Virgil trade looks.

                    BEBE
          Nature of the biz being what it is, why don't
          we just go for it? Do it together?

                    DANNY
          What're you suggesting? A menage à trois?

Danny frowns and Virgil half-smiles.

                    BEBE
          No, you idiots! Collaboration! On a
          rewrite!

Danny's uncertain. Virgil pipes in. Waving the script.

                    VIRGIL
          We could be a package. I know you know,
          Danny, that the best writing happens in the
          rewriting.

Bebe flirts up to Danny.

                    BEBE
          So what do you say? Still got that itch?

                    DANNY
          Don't expect me to rewrite just for the sake
          of rewriting.

                    BEBE
          You shouldn't. You don't want to fix what's
          not broken. What you want to do is
          discipline yourself into objectivity.

Danny holds firm. His pistol still trained on Virgil.

                    BEBE
          Better tell him how to approach it.

                    VIRGIL
          Not without being on common ground. The gun,
          Danny. Delete it.

                    BEBE
              (sweetly)
          Pen's mightier than the sword.

                    VIRGIL
     Likewise, some would say, the word processor.

Danny looks at the gun. Considers.

The weapon disappears from his hand.

                    VIRGIL
               (relieved)
     Good choice.

                    DANNY
               (shrugging)
     Spec screenplay. Nothing, I guess, is set in
     stone.

                    VIRGIL
     You bet. Sometimes, you've got to step back
     from the work for a while.

                    BEBE
     Distance yourself from it.

Virgil puts Danny's screenplay on a chair between them.

                    DANNY
     What if you don't have the time?

                    BEBE
     Pretend you do. Look through that window to
     your imagination.

                    VIRGIL
     Read your screenplay over and over again.
     Give yourself a full set of development
     notes.

                    BEBE
     Be hard on yourself. But be fair.

                    VIRGIL
     Ask yourself tough questions as you read and
     compile notes. Like, does my screenplay —

                    DANNY
     My screenplay!

                    VIRGIL
     Right! That's what I meant. Does your
     screenplay clearly, actively show the
     protagonist's mission, and what's at stake?

Danny glances at his script on the chair.

BEBE

Runs to him, throwing her arms around him in a passionate
embrace.

                    BEBE
               (off screen)
          Likewise the antagonist.

DANNY

Shakes the image from his head. Glares at

VIRGIL

Who pulls Bebe from his arms.

Kisses her.

DANNY

Blinks that image away as well.

                    DANNY
          What other questions should I ask?

                    VIRGIL
          Is the dialogue always functional? Saying
          just enough, not too much or too little?

                    BEBE
          Is there enough conflict?

                    VIRGIL
          Does every scene have a character trying to
          achieve an objective?

                    BEBE
          Action, reaction, conflict! Is that character
          being met with some opposition?

                    VIRGIL
          Is the plot progression and content of scenes
          logical within the given concept?

                    BEBE
          Avoiding unneeded repetition.

Danny chuckles to himself.

                    DANNY
          Heard that one before.

                    VIRGIL
        Are you creating cliffhangers . . . ?

Danny looks out from the veranda. The scenery of the
night, the streets twenty stories below.

                    VIRGIL
        . . . forcing the reader to continuously ask,
        what is going to happen next?

No longer amused, Danny's eyes again fix on

VIRGIL

Bebe is in his arms. But she's frightened. Struggling.

                    BEBE
              (off screen)
        Are you writing cinematically?

DANNY

Cringes. The image evaporates.

                    DANNY
        Showing instead of telling, writing action
        instead of explanation?

                    BEBE
        Are key beats and plot points being hit?

                    DANNY
        Set up, Inciting Incident, Act One
        Reversal . . . ?

                    BEBE
        Midpoint, Act Two Reversal, Climax, and
        Resolution.

                    DANNY
        What is going to be the resolution of this
        one, Virg?

He evades the question.

                    VIRGIL
        Is the audience being shown something they've
        never seen before?

                    BEBE
        Can't see on their own?

                    VIRGIL
        Are they seeing something in a new light,
        that's not part of their own mundane world?

                    BEBE
Are there surprises? Twists along the way?

                    VIRGIL
Are things close enough to the edge . . . in
terms of dialogue and imagery and action
. . . to compel?

                    BEBE
But not repel!

Danny looks at his script.

                    VIRGIL
Give it several selective readings.

                    BEBE
Read only the slug lines. Ask if they're
correctly defining time and place?

                    VIRGIL
Read the descriptive action. Is it easy on
the eyes? Clearly written, with a strong
sense of urgency?

                    BEBE
Is it simple, active, concise?

                    VIRGIL
Occurring in the here and now while conveying
the essence of the story?

                    BEBE
Are you varying your verbs, and are they
always in the present tense?

Danny rubs his forehead.

                    DANNY
What can I do to enhance place, emotion,
visualization, and the plot progression?

A sudden, howling wind. Danny battles the gale,
desperately trying to free Bebe, Virgil locking her in
his grip.

                    BEBE
Terrific question to ask yourself!

Hail stones the size of golf balls begin to pummel them.

> BEBE
> Here's another: Is there anything that you
> can add to the descriptive action, to create
> more conflict?

A screeching

PTERODACTYL

Swoops down on Danny, fiercely snatching him off the
veranda.

DANNY

Rubs his forehead, dismissing the images. No more wind,
hail, or flying dinosaurs.

> DANNY
> It's all so overwhelming.

Just Virgil, Bebe, and him standing in the warm starry
night.

> VIRGIL
> Then read just the dialogue.

> BEBE
> As with action, can the essence of the movie
> be followed through it?

> VIRGIL
> Does it sound natural, within the given
> concept?

> BEBE
> And, at the same time, is it always
> functional?

> VIRGIL
> Is it visual? Experiential? Are other tales
> worth hearing unfolding within it?

> BEBE
> Does it help clarify character and
> relationship, tone, and plot?

> VIRGIL
> Does it provide, if necessary, foreshadowing,
> and exposition?

> BEBE
> Is it tense, witty, colorful?

                    VIRGIL
Expressing what might be conceived as
familiar, in unfamiliar ways?

                    BEBE
Avoiding show and tell, and being too on-the-
nose?

                    VIRGIL
Are the characters disagreeing, arguing,
offering differing points of view?

                    BEBE
Does what they say always generate conflict!?

                    DANNY
Hold on! Are we talking about the one I've
written? Or the one we're inhabiting?

Danny motions to their surroundings.

                    DANNY
Because the dialogue in this script is
pedantic as all hell.

                    VIRGIL
         (pointedly)
Which is why, Danny-boy, it'll never be made
into a movie.

Danny scratches his head.

                    VIRGIL
Read your leading characters one at a time.

                    BEBE
Track the protagonist. Antagonist.

                    VIRGIL
Are they proactive?

                    BEBE
Making active decisive choices when
confronted by obstacles?

                    VIRGIL
Are their arcs consistent with the way
they've been set up?

                    BEBE
Do they change and grow in credible ways?
Beginning, middle, and end?

                    VIRGIL
     Do they achieve their objectives and
     missions? Is it clear why they have or have
     not?

                    BEBE
     Is there reason to care?

Danny gazes at Bebe.

                    DANNY
     Is there?

Her tender smile is the answer. Virgil shoots them a
subtle, sinister look.

                    VIRGIL
     Read key supporting characters.

                    BEBE
     Ask, are they making adequate appearances in
     all three acts? Or have they been neglected?

                    DANNY
     I'd never neglect you, Bebe.

                    VIRGIL
     Are each one of them needed or just excess
     baggage?

                    BEBE
     Are they contributing to the plot?

                    VIRGIL
     Helping define one of the leads?

                    BEBE
     Can they be merged with another character?
     Or be deleted, without being missed?

Danny holds out his hand.

                    DANNY
     No one could ever take your place.

Bebe puts hers out, as well. Ready to clasp his.

                    VIRGIL
     Do they bring something exciting to the page?

                    BEBE
     Can you further color any or all of your
     characters?

>   VIRGIL
>   Give them unexpected traits and or
>   activities? To enhance them in our mind's
>   eye?

Danny pauses. He notices, in the moonlight, that Virgil
has two tiny horns peering through his thinning hair.

>   VIRGIL
>   Ask yourself what can be done to bring them
>   out of the realm of the obvious?

A wicked grin creases his lips.

>   VIRGIL
>   I know what you're thinking, Danny. Remember
>   what I said about omnipotence?

>   DANNY
>   Yeah. But it's my screenplay.

>   VIRGIL
>   As if.

He snatches Danny's script off the lounge.

>   VIRGIL
>   I'm doing the rewrite.

>   DANNY
>   Not on your life!

>   VIRGIL
>   Then what about Bebe's!?

He grabs her. She screams.

>   VIRGIL
>   Surrender the property to me, bro.

Danny starts to reach for her. But Virgil whips the
script up to her neck.

>   VIRGIL
>   Or I'll paper-cut her throat.

Danny hesitates. Uncertain what to do.

>   BEBE
>   He's bluffing, Danny.
>   (to Virgil)
>   You know I'm the element needed to get this
>   project made.

                    VIRGIL
          Talk about inflated egos. Simple revision,
          romantic interest becomes a dog.

Bebe and Danny exchange subtle nods. He lunges for
Virgil as Bebe tries to snatch the script.

Virgil wrestles them for it. Falls backward.

                    DANNY
          Bebe!

Danny leaps toward

THE EDGE

Grabbing Bebe by the hand as she tumbles off the veranda
with Virgil.

Bebe dangles over the edge. One hand holding Danny's.
The other, his script. Virgil hangs below her. Gripping
his end of the screenplay.

Danny tries to pull them up. Together, they're too
heavy.

                    DANNY
          Let go of my script, Hans — I mean, Virgil.

Virgil looks down. Twenty stories to the cars,
sidewalks, and pedestrians. The script begins to tear.

                    VIRGIL
          Gotta be kidding me.

                    DANNY
          Bebe! Let it go!

                    BEBE
               (breathy, melodramatic)
          No way, Danny. It is too important to you.
          To me. To the future of American Cinema.

The script rips in half.

Virgil screams. Plummeting downward as Danny yanks Bebe
back up on the veranda.

INT. BACHELOR PAD — LATE NIGHT

Danny's head bolts up from his desk. Shaken. Suddenly
awake at his computer.

The moon casts amber light through the window. Crossing
the corner of a shadowed poster for a movie starring Bebe
La Rue, Hollywood goddess from an era long gone.

> LADY LOVE
> (off screen)
> Come to bed?

He looks over his shoulder. Wipes the sleep from his
eyes.

Alluring in lingerie, his LADY LOVE leans against the
bedroom door.

> LADY LOVE
> Finish the revisions tomorrow?

> DANNY
> In a few. Still grappling with the
> resolution.

She curls her lip in an enticing pout.

> LADY LOVE
> You know where to find me. If you could use a
> little inspiration.

Saunters back into the bedroom.

Danny considers. And cockily grins.

He gets up. Swaggers toward the bedroom.

But pauses. Turns. Drawn like a magnet to

THE COMPUTER

A page from his screenplay hums on the monitor.

FADE TO BLACK

The End.